"The power of fasting with prayer is biblical (*Matthew 17:20 from the St. Joseph Bible, New Edition*). Jesus said that there are certain demons that cannot be cast out but through prayer and fasting. The two are a powerful team and Andy LaVallee, through his book, provides us with means to accomplish this goal." Jim and Kerri Caviezel

"Andy LaVallee has provided the method, the motive and the means for the spiritual discipline of fasting. His book explains why fasting is important and encourages many to take part in this vital aspect of spiritual warfare in the world today."
Fr. Dwight Longenecker, Pastor, Speaker, Blogger and Author of *Mystery of the Magi: the Quest to Identify the Three Wise Men*

"Andy LaVallee is a man of deep faith and conviction. His life lived in commitment to prayer and fasting has resulted in a generous witness to the Church. Andy desires that all people come to know God's benevolent love and the intercessory power of our Blessed Mother. This book is one of his many efforts to evangelize us all in the tradition of *living the fast*. I have always been grateful for his passion for the Gospel, his commitment to the Church, and his tireless endeavors in helping us all grow in holiness."
Fr. Ross Chamberland, O.F.M.

"Today we are horrified by increasing incidences of bloodshed as our world descends into darkness and despair of healing our broken hearts. In this book, LaVallee powerfully explains by using traditional Catholic teaching, Scriptures and personal testimony, that a relationship with Jesus contains the healing we are seeking and that fasting combined with prayer is the most powerful means of conversion for us and for the world."
Leticia Velasquez, author, founder of KIDS, *Keep Kids With Down Syndrome*

"Jesus really HAS provided the solution, and Andy tells it like it is! This book absolutely HAD to be written and I am profoundly grateful that Andy was chosen to write it!   It is easy to read and full of grace. Thank you, Andy, for this powerful weapon. I look forward to arming my parishioners with it."
Fr. Anthony Cipolle, M.Div.   St. Paul the Apostle Parish, Bangor, Maine

When You Fast

Jesus Has Provided the Solution

by

Andrew LaVallee

Live the Fast
Waltham, MA

Published on the Feast of Our Lady of Guadalupe, December 12, 2017

Editing/ formatting by
Ellen Gable Hrkach

To purchase additional copies go to:
http://www.livethefast.org

Dedicated to:

Our Lady, the Mother of God
"The world is on the edge of catastrophe...
to avoid this, the whole world is invited to pray and fast."
Our Lady of Kibeho,
Vatican-approved apparition,
August 1982

To the healing of all families
who pray and fast

Table of Contents

Foreword

"Fasting gives birth to prophets and strengthens the powerful; fasting makes lawgivers wise. Fasting is a good safeguard for the soul, a steadfast companion for the body, a weapon for the valiant, and a gymnasium for athletes. Fasting repels temptations, anoints unto piety; it is the comrade of watchfulness and the artificer of chastity. In war it fights bravely, in peace it teaches stillness." Saint Basil the Great

The message that comes from Medjugorje to the whole world is simple and yet very powerful. Those who have embraced this core message coming from Our Lady, Queen of Peace, immediately find that the road to holiness becomes attainable, but at the same time, the spiritual warfare intensifies.

The central part of the message is based upon five stones which Our Lady recommends to use against our Goliath, namely: prayer, fasting, the Bible, Confession, and the Eucharist. Of these five, the least-known spiritual weapon is certainly fasting. For us Westerners, it is not as essential as it has been for our brothers and sisters in the East for centuries, yet those who discover the benefits of this spiritual practice will soon realize that their efforts to attain holiness of life become more concrete and reachable.

In this book, Andy LaVallee shares with all of us a beautiful journey that led him to discover the incredible benefits of fasting, as well as a call that he received to make Our Lady's wishes known throughout the world.

More and more we need to incorporate this beautiful practice of fasting into our spiritual toolbox.

In the Old Testament and in the New Testament, there are many examples of fasting. Jesus fasted frequently. According to Tradition, fasting is encouraged, especially in times of great temptation or severe trials. Certain devils, said Jesus, *"can be cast out in no other way except by prayer and fasting"* (Mark 9:29).

Fasting is essential in order to achieve spiritual freedom. Through fasting, one is better able to listen to God and man and to perceive them more clearly. If, through fasting, we achieve that freedom, we will be more aware of many things. Once we are aware that we can enjoy the necessities of life without struggle, then many fears and worries fade away. We become more open to our families and to the people with whom we live and work. Our Lady recommends fasting twice a week: *"Fast strictly on Wednesdays and Fridays"* (August 14, 1984).

She asks us to accept this difficult message *"...with a firm will."* She asks us to *"persevere in ... fasting"* (June 25, 1982).

She says that "the best fast is on bread and water. Through fasting and prayer one can stop wars, one can suspend the natural laws of nature. Works of charity cannot replace fasting....Everyone, except the sick, has to fast" (July 21, 1982).

We have to realize the power of fasting. Fasting means to make a sacrifice to God, to offer not only our prayers, but also to make our whole being participate in sacrifice. We should fast with love, for a special intention, and to purify ourselves and the world. We should fast because we love God and want to be soldiers that offer our bodies in the battle against evil.

Are you struggling with a sin? I mean a sin that you just can't seem to get rid of, a sin that keeps you in a constant state of guilt and despair. You've prayed, you've frequented the sacraments, but you just can't seem to break its hold.

We've all been there at one point or another, and such struggles are part and parcel of the spiritual life. But it doesn't have to be that way. In this book, Andy LaVallee introduces us to a very powerful but much neglected weapon in the spiritual arsenal: Fasting.

If you want to energize your spiritual life, if you want to slay a sin that has you in bondage, if you want to grow in union with God, take up the holy weapon of fasting. For as Jesus said, I repeat, there are some demons that cannot be driven out by anything but prayer and fasting.

So, open your mind and heart as you read these pages. A mother always knows what is best for her children; trust Our Lady when she invites us to fast and pray. To make fasting easier, **she has given us also the Chaplet of Holy Fast**. Learn it, pray it, use it -- and prepare yourself to reach new levels of closeness to God that you had never experienced before.

If we neglect fasting, our spiritual life will always be mediocre. We will be weak in the combat against our passions, we will easily succumb to temptation, and we will never truly overcome our inherent selfishness and self-indulgence.

As men and women of this century, our desire should be to strengthen ourselves and be the best that we can be. We should train ourselves to be strong in the spiritual warfare, so we can resist the temptations of the Evil One. There is no better way to begin this spiritual training than through the practice of fasting.

Rev. Francisco J. Anzoategui Peiro
Pastor, Saint Stephen Parish, Framingham, MA

Introduction

Why A Catholic Book on Fasting?

How can fasting change lives? When people pray and fast, Christ works miracles in people's souls. He works miracles when people pray *and* fast.

After writing *From the Hub to the Heart*, I never thought I would write another book. However, fasting has had such an enormous impact on my life — going from a life of sin to a soldier in Our Lady's Army — that I felt compelled to share my thoughts and experiences on how this discipline can heal *all* wounds.

There are many good books on fasting from a Protestant perspective. But there aren't very many fasting books from a Catholic perspective.

As a golfer pre-conversion, one of my favorite books was Ben Hogan's *The Modern Fundamentals of Golf*. This book, written in 1957, has been a must read for any golfer at any level. My friend Charlie Fox clarified it when he said, "You need to write a book on the fundamentals of fasting and how it changed your life."

So why is a guy in the bakery business promoting fasting? First, because I know breads; success in fasting depends on success on the kinds of breads with which you fast.

Our Lady has repeatedly told us through many Church-approved apparitions that we need to pray AND fast. Our world is in deep trouble. It's going to take a miracle to change our world. That's where fasting comes in. With fasting, we can make the impossible, possible.

There are so many spiritual and medical benefits to fasting. Fasting is important, not only to *my* life but to *everyone's* life.

Our Lady in her reported apparition in Medjugorje on January 25th, 2001, said this: "Dear children! Today I call you to renew prayer and fasting with even greater enthusiasm until prayer becomes a joy for you. Little children, the one who prays is not afraid of the future and the one who fasts is not afraid of evil. Once again, I repeat to you: only through prayer and fasting also wars can be stopped – wars of your unbelief and fear for the future."

Finally, many points are purposely repeated in this book to drive the message home, but this book is all about "when you fast," how you fast and what might happen to your life when you start fasting.

Prologue

Conversion Story and Medjugorje

In the spring of 2010, I was going to Sunday Mass pretty regularly. I had been teaching C.C.D. for boys for ten years at Saint Charles in Waltham, for Father Copp, but he would be really terrified if he knew the kind of life I was living as I was teaching the boys about the Holy Spirit, the Sacraments, and the saints! I was going to Mass but, as I learned later, I was not receiving the Holy Eucharist in a state of grace. Still, there were times as a C.C.D. teacher that I felt I was 'in the zone.' I would go into class, without notes prepared, and stuff would just flow and it would be a great class. So here I was, considering attending the Boston Catholic Men's Conference, but since I had never gone to conferences or retreats, I was unsure whether I should go. My friend Joe said, "You should go, and bring your son Jeff."

So we went to the conference, and the keynote speaker was Jim Caviezel. At the time, I hadn't seen *The Passion of the Christ*, so I had no idea who Jim was. He opened up his talk saying, "I always love coming to Boston because of the 1980 Olympic Hockey Team beating the big, bad Russians. They taught me to believe in miracles. Most of those players were from Boston. I keep telling my agent, 'I'd love to meet those guys.' I don't know what it is, but he's never put me in touch with them." So he continued with his talk, and I was saying to myself, "He wants to meet those guys; I grew up with the best one!" Jack O'Callahan (O.C.) and I had been friends for fifty years; we grew up a few blocks from each other. So I gave my card to one of the event organizers, and next thing I knew, the conference ended and I was sitting at a table with Jim Caviezel, Cardinal Sean O'Malley, and my son Jeff. Jim was asking me questions about the guys on the Olympic Hockey Team. He told me that when he watched the 1980 team, it had a big impact on his life and career.

Then he said, "By the way, you have to come to Medjugorje with me this summer." I responded, "Hey, Jim, I have no idea what Medjugorje is." Then I looked at Tim Van Damm who was standing a few feet away. He was Jim's assistant during that weekend. Jim was with his wife Kerry for that whole weekend as he spoke to the Men's Conference; she addressed the Women's Conference. So Jim repeated, "You're coming to Medjugorje with me this summer!" I replied, "Look, Jim, don't get your hopes up, because I'm not flying fifteen hours to pray a Rosary!" Looking back and remembering that I said that in front of the Cardinal, it was probably not the best idea! So as we left, Jim said, "We're going to get together; we're going to become friends." I said, "Whatever," and I left thinking, "Can you imagine this guy saying we are going to become friends? He's a movie star in Hollywood, and I'm from Charlestown and he's going to become friends with me? Why would a guy who played Jesus Christ in a big-time movie want to become friends with me?"

The next day, I was running a little late, and the cell phone beeped. It was an eight-minute voicemail from Jim Caviezel. I came home and started listening to it. Jim was saying the same thing. "You have to go to Medjugorje, and Kerry's speaking today. Please come to the Women's Conference." I thought, "No way, I'm not going over there." So I played golf instead.

Then one day as I was visiting a customer in Everett,

the next town over from Charlestown, my car was detoured up Bunker Hill Street, where I lived until I was nineteen. As I was driving up the street, I reflected to myself. "Boy, I have not been here in years." Then my cell phone rang. I tried to answer it, but there was static on the line and was not clear. I started to get a clearer signal, so I pulled over and parked. It was Jim. "Hey, Andy, are we going to Medjugorje in June? It's the last chance for you to come." That's when I looked up. I couldn't believe it. I had parked in front of the statue of the Blessed Mother where I prayed as I walked to and from school each day. I was a little stunned, so I found myself saying, "Okay. I will be there. When can we meet?" Jim asked, "What changed your mind?" I replied, "I will let you know when I see you in person."

I thought, *I don't know what this means, but I guess I am going on a pilgrimage for the first time in my life*. I just sensed it. I didn't know what to think, but I felt peace in it. There was something in me which said, 'You better do this.' When that happened to me in my life, it was usually a pretty good sign, yet this was a different feeling. It was not the same business instinct, yet I still felt that I had to listen.

So I called Tim and I said, "Guess what? We're going to Medjugorje!" He asked, "What do you mean we're going to Medjugorje?" I replied, "I just told Caviezel I would go, but I am not going without you." So he said, "Are you asking or telling?" I said, "Telling." He answered, "Okay. I'm in."

I found out later this was going to be Caviezel's seventh trip. On the flight over, I was reading Jan Connell's book *Queen of the Cosmos*. It captivated me so much that I silently contemplated having a life confession in Medjugorje. I started wondering, "Can the Blessed

Mother really be appearing there? Come on, is it really true? If it's true, then I have a lot of cleaning up to do!" In the last five years, I had been to confession infrequently, but they were not very good confessions, or even worthy of God's mercy. I was a self-employed businessman filled with pride, and assumed that all the crime, violence and sin throughout my life could not be forgiven.

So the car pulled up to the hotel in Medjugorje and we checked into our rooms. We were staying right next to Ivan's chapel, looking right up a mountain. I asked Tim, "What's that crucifix up there?" He answered, "Oh, that's Cross Mountain, a thirty-foot high white cement crucifix with a relic of the original cross inside it." I said, "Tim, it's two different colors." He asked, "What do you mean?" I replied, "It's blue, white, blue, white." He said, "I don't see blue, white, and blue, white." And then he stopped and said, "Oh wait, now it is blue, white, blue, white." I asked, "Is someone up there filming a movie or something?" He shook his head. "There's nothing up there, no electricity, nothing. Andy, this is a Medjugorje wakeup call." I replied, "Yeah, we'll see." I didn't believe it.

The next day we met with Jim Caviezel. I gave him an autographed picture of my friend Jack O' Callahan and he loved it. Then we walked through the fields in order to go to Mass. It felt really odd, not like the plush fairways I was used to, not even like the busy sidewalks of Boston. I did not tell anybody during the walk, but I was filled with anticipation, and my heart was pounding as we prayed a Rosary together.

We met up with Jim after Holy Mass, and he said, "We're going across the street to Colombo's for brunch. Why don't you guys join us?" First Tim and I walked to

Leo's Jewelry Store, a few hundred yards away, to get a four-way medal similar to what Tim was wearing. I had not worn a religious medal since my mom made me wear one years ago. Tim thought it was important so I agreed to get one. We walked up the street to join Jim for lunch and as we approached the table, I saw Jim at a big round table holding court with six priests. Tim and I joined them, and we made it a party of nine. There was delicious-looking Croatian food everywhere; it was like a big feast. One of the priests, Father Michael Lightner, was sitting directly across from me. No lightweight at six feet, four inches, about 330 pounds, Fr. Michael played college and pro football and had worked security for the band U2.

Father Michael was telling everyone at the table about his conversion in Medjugorje. He was all banged up, with bruises and bandages like he got beat up in a bad street fight and I thought, "This guy is full of it." Later I learned that he had just had a bad motorcycle spill. Then the topic switched to his conversion in Medjugorje. In his younger days, his mom Joyce found some drugs in his duffle bag and was so upset that she forced him to go with her to Medjugorje. When he arrived there, Father Michael challenged God, saying, "If you exist, I do not know You. You got one week to show me who You are. After that, I am out of here!" That one phrase made me believe him and his story. He told us about his life confession and spoke of confessing major sins like alcohol, drugs, pornography and many more. After his confession, he said he felt this pressure pinning him back in the confessional and he thought, "Okay, God, I believe you're real!"

Father Michael looked directly at me. "I know you're a friend of Jim's, but what are you doing here, Andy?" I replied, "Father Michael, I really don't know." He said,

"For me, when I got away from all that rubbish, it started in confession, and if you haven't been in a while, you might need a life confession."

It was like somebody took a sword and pierced me right in my heart, like God was saying to me, "I'm asking you to do this *right now*." I said to myself, "Come on, this isn't possible. Can God really be telling me to do this?" Then the Charlestown side of me came out, and this is what was going on in my mind. I looked at the table, there were several bottles of wine and delicious food and the guy who was sitting across from me — he might be a priest but he weighs 330 pounds — and I told myself, "There's no way he's getting up from this table! Look at this stuff, look at the cutlets, he's not leaving this!" So sure in my mind that it was not going to happen, I turned to him. "Father Michael, I just contemplated a life confession on the way here. You might even know that. Let's go do a confession right now." He said, "Okay, let's go." Now I was really convinced I had to do this!

We got up from that beautiful table and went across the street to Saint James' Church. He walked into the sacristy, put on his vestments, got two chairs, then carefully put them closely facing each other as we sat down. He took so much care in placing these chairs that I was starting to ask myself, "Will he pay that much attention to my sins?" Then I began, "Bless me, Father, for I have sinned." He said, "Hold on, this is what we are going to do. You give me your sins by the decade, from 0-10 years, 10-20 years, 20-30 years and so on, each decade that you lived; the things you did, what you were challenged with, thinking about, everything. I want to know everything, don't hold anything back. Give me everything."

So then I start with ages 0-10; I stole some candy bars, beat up my brother and disrespected this one, that one. Then, between ages 10 and 20, I stole some money from my parents' dresser, stole a car, broke into a house. I was getting into some serious sins. I was not holding back. From ages 20 to 30, I laid it all on the line and during ages 40 to 50, he said, "Okay. I get it; here is what's going on. All your sins are sins of abandonment. Has anybody really close to you died in your life?"

I thought, "This is starting to get really scary. He is a mind reader!" So then I told him all about my dad. This went on for two and a half hours and, by the end, I was bawling; my clothes were soaked with my tears. I was exhausted, but I never felt better in my entire life! I didn't need Lufthansa to get home; I could have flown home on my own! So we started to wrap it up when I took the four-way medal out of my pocket that I bought earlier at Leo's, and asked him to bless it and put it on me. So he said, "Hold on to it; I am going to give you absolution, I want you to understand some things might happen that you've never experienced before, so don't freak out on me." I didn't know what he meant. So for whatever reason, he wanted to prepare me for what I was about to experience. He said "Bow your head." We were sitting knee to knee, me and this man whom I now felt not only represents God but has direct access to Him. He placed his fist on my chest, he had his other hand on my forehead, and I felt like someone had just turned an iron on, his hand was so hot. He was hitting me in the chest with his fist, praying, "Almighty Father, I pray to You to soften this man's heart." Father was praying to the Lord for me, he was giving me absolution, and I was sitting there with my hands folded. I was listening, saying to myself, "What the heck's going on here?" I was starting to

21

doubt. Then, for the first time in my life, I heard someone speaking in tongues, but when I focused on my heart and God, and trusted, suddenly I heard him speaking in English, loud and clear.

Between the speaking in tongues and the heat of his hand on my head, I had never experienced anything like this before. We finished the confession. I handed him the medal, and he reached for a black pouch beside him filled with bottles of blessed oil. He then blessed the medal with holy water and holy oil and placed it around my neck, and it's never been off my neck since then. You could give me a million dollars in cash and I would not take this medal off!

I walked away from confession and I knelt in the stones and dust behind Saint James Church, and prayed my penance of seven hundred seventy Our Fathers, slow and from the heart, just like Father Michael said. I learned a couple of things. Father Michael didn't just give me the Sacrament of Confession. He taught me all the reasons why I was acting out in the sins I was committing. He told me that they were sins of abandonment; I was missing the love of my father, because he abandoned me, not only for the times he left me in the car, or failed to show up at my sporting events, but from his heart attack and death. I really needed him to be there, and he wasn't, and I had to forgive him for that. I had to forgive myself for what I had done to him, because I had carried that with me for thirty-five years. Once I was able to forgive my father, and myself, I would be able to receive the Lord's full mercy and forgiveness for everything I had done. Then, most importantly, when I was given that opportunity to do it for other people, I had to do the same. God was showing me His example of forgiveness through this amazing sacrament, and I needed to embrace this forgiveness. This was going to be the center of my relationship with Our Lord. He was going to teach me the power of love and forgiveness.

I knelt behind Saint James Church, with two hands on the wooden bench for support; I was soaked in perspiration, and it was painful. As I prayed the Our Father, as slowly as I have ever prayed it, I felt the presence of our loving Mother. She was there to comfort me just as she did her Son. Even though I looked like I had just fallen out of a dumpster, and there were many people walking by me, nobody stopped to see if I was all right. To them, it was just another stunning conversion in the miraculous village of Medjugorje.

From the time I left the table at Colombo's, I was gone for almost six hours, so I returned to the hotel afterwards. Tim asked, "What the heck happened? Where have you been? You look like you've seen a ghost!" And I replied, "Tim, I had a life confession, you won't believe it." He said, "I believe it. Why do you think Our Lady invited you here?" We got to talking and I told him the whole story. I had learned an awful lot through this experience and so I began to think, "*Now* I can be in the presence of the Blessed Mother."

The next day we went right up to pray the Stations at Cross Mountain. Tim and his friend Sean walked up barefoot. I had enough trouble doing it with sneakers on! We prayed and cried and when we reached the top, it was beautiful. I really did not want to leave.

Tim knew the visionary Ivan, and we went to his chapel every day and, within two nights, Ivan invited us to accompany him as he had a private apparition. We went to see visionary Vicka in the village and she prayed over me. Two days later, it was 100 degrees, and we were on

Apparition Hill. Usually, I would have been at the beach or in the pool in weather like this, and I thought to myself, "What am I doing here, praying between two mountains?" I was trying to follow what was happening. We were going up the rocky hill in the heat to pray the Rosary. We walked up the Joyful Mystery side; there were about 100 people there. Maria Paulic, owner of the Two Hearts Hotel (where we were staying) led a group from Ohio and we decided to join them. As we were going up the hill, I got separated from the group. I saw Tim on the side. I walked around another larger group to get further up the hill. Then I saw a woman sitting on a rock and she had a stack of file cards. I know now that they were prayer intentions. She was older, about seventy, and she looked kind of sickly, so I glanced down and I asked her, "Are you okay?" She stared at me and said, "Give me your hand, young man." So I gave her my hand and pulled her up. She said, "You are going to help me up this hill to visit Our Lady and bring her these prayer intentions." Now, I had recent back problems that had prevented me from playing golf, and it had never entered my mind to help her. But I said to myself, "I just got to help this lady." So this forty-minute journey from the bottom of the hill to the statue of Our Lady turned into a two-and-a-half-hour excursion. I met Tim about three-quarters of the way up the hill as he was helping this woman's friend. The two of us were helping these women up the hill.

When we got there, we were exhausted. I said to Tim, "All well and good. We got them up here, but how the heck are we going to get them down?" I was worried because I figured it would be harder getting them down. Tim replied, "Just pray." I said, "Come on!" He responded, "Just do what I am telling you to do. Trust in the Lord." I said, "Okay."

After hours in the heat assisting these women, we got them down the hill, they thanked us, and we walked away feeling like we had just helped these ladies do something very special.

The next day at the hotel, we went downstairs for breakfast — well, not really breakfast, just bread and water because it was a Friday and that's a fasting day in Medjugorje. The woman I helped up and down the hill was giving testimony about her pilgrimage to forty people over breakfast. It turns out that she had been sick and was talking about meeting this man on Apparition Hill who was her guardian angel helping her take her prayer intentions to Our Lady.   I was standing behind her, and she didn't know I was there. I said to myself, "You've got to be kidding me!" I took a few moments to gather myself. Tim and I were going to sit at another table a few feet away, then she stopped talking and she shouted, "There's my guardian angel!" And she introduced me to everybody in her group and I was crying again. Even though my parents had both died young, God had given me the opportunity to be a son again to a woman I didn't even know. God was asking me to serve her, to help her and to test me to see if I was going to listen to His inspiration and obey, or if I was going to walk away. So I said, "Okay. God forgave me in confession, I did this act of service for her, and then I was rewarded because when I came into that room, she was speaking about me." That tied it all in for me, what I had done with a simple "Yes." God can do a lot with a simple "Yes" from us.

The third big event on my first trip to Medjugorje happened when I was introduced to the writings of Father Slavko Barbaric about fasting. Neither fasting nor Medjugorje was ever on my radar before. However, in fasting, I had found a practice that assisted me both spiritually and physically on this pilgrimage, so I felt compelled to learn more about it. I wondered, "How come the rest of the church is not practicing it, especially if the Blessed Mother is recommending it?" I started reading about fasting a few days before we returned home. The best books written were by Father Slavko, and in Medjugorje, the people there told me he held many fasting retreats until his death in November of 2000.

Then, on our last night in Medjugorje, I was sitting on the porch overlooking Apparition Hill at three a.m. I heard a group of Italian women a few feet below, singing the *Ave Maria* while praying the Rosary and I decided to join them. So I sat with them to pray, and then I felt like I was getting some kind of a message from above. "Fasting breads," I heard. Again, I heard in my heart the term, "fasting breads." I asked myself, "What is a 'fasting bread?'"

On the flight home, when Tim and I were returning from our trip, there were many thoughts racing through my head. He begged me to let him sleep, but I kept poking him every time I read something else amazing about fasting. My entire world view had changed, leaving so many burning questions demanding an answer: How would I describe my experience to my family back home? Why am I living at this time in history? What is my purpose in life? What did God create me for? How am I to re-pay God? When can I come back to Medjugorje? The biggest question which remained in my mind was: What on earth is 'fasting bread'? You would think that after thirty-eight years in the bakery industry, I would understand this term!

As I pondered the incredible changes that occurred in me during my miraculous week in Medjugorje, I knew one thing for sure. Although I only realized it then, at age fifty-five, Our Lady's guiding hand had been upon me since my childhood. She was there when my mom asked me to pray a Hail Mary on my walk to Saint Francis De Sales School. Her statue on my path to school was a reminder of her loving protection, even though I was barely aware of it as I passed by. I took my faith for granted as I grew up, involved in the violent life of Charlestown, but she was there, interceding for me. Our Lady was calling me while I worked around the clock to build my business and pursue fame at the racetrack. She continued to wait patiently for me, as I attended Mass sporadically and left early when it interfered with my golf game. Slowly and surely, I recognized her gentle motherly influence in my life, though if you had asked me at that time, I couldn't have told you why I began to attend Mass more regularly. I didn't know why I began a relationship with Fr. Copp, but My Mother did. I now know that Our Lady, Mother Mary, was behind my decision to accept the challenge of teaching C.C.D. to rowdy adolescent boys. Our Lady used Jim Caviezel, who gave her his heart and his acting career, to issue a challenge to me, who never was known to refuse a challenge, to go to an obscure village in Croatia to pray. It was there, at the foot of her statue, the statue which overlooked my childhood that I finally surrendered to her gentle power, saying "Yes" to coming to Medjugorje. Tim Van Damm was there to guide me to Medjugorje to the table where Father Michael Lightner accepted my challenge to leave a feast, and help me go through a life confession. Our Lady had orchestrated it all out of her love for me.

Our Lady has a way of showing us a different path, and she certainly did with me. I am forever grateful for her love, and for the direction she used to bring me back to her Son. The best advice I got to try and to reflect and answer these questions was from Jim Caviezel, who said, "Have patience and trust in God, but most of all, you now can follow the peace in your heart. You are part of Our Lady's Plan."

The following is a reflection from my first trip to Medjugorje and my first experience with fasting.

2010

Today is our third day here in Medjugorje, and it's time to climb Cross Mountain. This is the highest mountain in the region and it is called Mount Krizevac by the villagers, meaning "Mount of the Cross." In 1933, the parish of St. James built a large concrete cross to venerate the 1900th Anniversary of Jesus' Passion and Death on the cross, and a relic of the True Cross of Jesus was built into this cross. It takes about two hours to climb this mountain, as you climb, you pray the 14 Stations of the Cross. There have been countless recorded healings and conversions at the foot of the cross.

How can we possibly climb this mountain without any food or breakfast? Today is Wednesday and in Medjugorje, it's a fast day and eating consists of only bread and water for 24 hours. What? We are going climb the largest mountain in the area and pray without any breakfast or protein and energy except for wholegrain bread and some water?

Today will be a totally different and new experience for me. It will be an athletic event of mountain climbing with no food; only bread and water. Fasting is part of Our Lady's messages, and I told our small group that I would try fasting on Wednesday and Friday. So why do we have

28

to climb the mountain today? Why not climb it on a Thursday when we have full nutrition? Without proper nutrition, this event will be impossible.

We are walking along the main street in Medjugorje, just after the ten a.m. English Mass. Our journey will take us to the base of the mountain to start our climb. As we pass each open- air market and coffee stand -- and even a bakery -- in my mind, I entertain the idea of breaking the fast before I even get started. I just had a life confession two days ago. Perhaps I can break the fast without anyone seeing me. The Holy Spirit finally gets the better of me, and I decide that some things are best left unsaid. The life confession is a new start.

According to my friend, Tim (who has been here many times), Cross Mountain is one of the most important things you can do while on pilgrimage in Medjugorje. It's the actual climb that makes pilgrims reflect on their relationship with Jesus, not the 5500 feet of stone-filled rocky terrain that one has to travel to get to the foot of the cross.

So off we go with a bottle of water in one hand and a loaf of wholegrain bread to share among four guys in the other. Tim has the yellow prayer book entitled, "The Stations of the Cross," by Father Tomislav Ivancic, a Medjugorje priest. The book has all 14 stations numbered, a reflection, and then one of Our Lady's Messages. (NB: Medjugorje is an ongoing apparition, so the Church has not yet recognized it as an authentic apparition site.)

Between my life confession and watching the people climb Apparition Hill and Cross Mountain barefoot, I think it's clear that most people who come here believe that Our Lady is appearing.

When we get to the fifth station, Tim hands me the yellow book and says, "Andy, you read and pray."

The fifth station is 'Simon of Cyrene helps Jesus carry the cross.' As I take the book, I cannot help but feel an adrenaline rush that gives me the sense that we just climbed up to the fifth station, and I am not tired or weak at all. In fact, each reflection that we read, regardless of the tears that are falling, gives me more energy than I have ever had before. Maybe there is something to this fasting thing, I think.

We get to the area marked by a stone before the top of the mountain where on November 24th, 2000, Father Slavko Barbaric died at 3.30 in the afternoon. He had just prayed the Way of the Cross with the pilgrims like he normally did, felt some pain in his chest, and dropped to the ground and died. The thought comes over me that I want to learn as much as I can about this priest. As it turns out, Father Slavko was a champion of fasting and has written many books on the topic. I tell Tim that whenever we get off this mountain, I am going to the Franciscan bookstore and buy his books.

The climb is over. We have returned to the bottom of the mountain, and I am totally astonished with my first encounter with the discipline of prayer and fasting. Why don't more people fast? I know we have plans of breaking the fast at midnight tonight with a few pints and pizza with Father Michael, but I really need to learn more about why this was so easy for me.

Our pilgrimage has reached its last day and I know people at home are going to ask, how was it? All I can say is the trip was life-changing. As we board the plane to return to Boston, I have my brown book on fasting written by Father Slavko, a bunch of yellow highlighters, and I am *determined to learn about this priest and about fasting.*

Tim, the organizer of the trip, is exhausted and wants to sleep, and presses his head against the window, as we fall into a two-seated aisle where we are both sitting. We are about 15 minutes into the flight when I read, "The spiritual role of fasting is misunderstood and therefore not taught or practiced." I nudge Tim with my elbow to tell him what I just discovered. He says "LaVal, please let me sleep." So I mark it with my highlighter. The more I read, the more I want to elbow Tim and ask him how come more people do not fast. Our Lady and Father Slavko have something here.

Chapter One

Why Fast?

"So we fasted, seeking this from our God,
and it was granted." (Ezra 8:23)

One of the first stories I ever heard about the power of prayer combined with the discipline of fasting was back in 2011. I had just returned to Medjugorje. I met and spent time with Sister Emmanuel Maillard (a religious sister who has written books on fasting). She told me the following story:

There was a teenage boy who had a deep wound and infection in his leg. He decided to go to the doctor, and the doctor took one look at it and sent him directly to the specialist. The specialist ordered some tests and sent them to the lab. After a few days, the boy's leg got worse, but he became hopeful with news from the doctor: "Young man, I just got your tests back and I want you to know that I have the cure for your infection, but I must explain that this cure is twofold and must be used together. If you use these two remedies together, your leg will be totally 100% healed."

This is exactly how prayer and fasting work; both are extremely powerful together. Prayer and fasting can totally heal all our wounds and all the wounds in the world today. Sister Emmanuel told me, "Andrew, we must be willing to sacrifice by fasting and combining it with prayer."

Fasting brings our life of prayer to a deeper level of spirituality. When I fast, I can tell you that the answers to my prayers from Our Lord come much more quickly. Prayer and fasting can be used for us and for the spiritual benefit of those we love who may not be practicing our faith, or for those in need we don't even know.

Also, what Sister Emmanuel was alluding to in her story is that we have come to the point in history that only heaven can cure us. As Father John Ricardo says, "There must be a radical return to God."

Imagine that you're one of the original twelve apostles, and you have learned your craft directly from Jesus Himself. The lessons and teachings you have learned can be taken right to the street to be passed on successfully to all those you touch through Jesus and His ministry. However, what happens in the story of the apostles casting out a demon in the boy in Matthew's Gospel (17)? The disciples are unsuccessful in applying their craft, and they cannot cast out the demon. So they return to the Master. "Why, Lord, can we not do this?" This is kind of like us today. If you are like me, you are always asking yourself, "Why? Why? Why?" Jesus responds to the apostles, "nothing is impossible for you but this kind *can only come out by prayer and fasting."*

So much is contained in this short Scripture statement of Jesus. First, I have learned — and have the faith through my own experience — that it needs to be understood that some demons or addictions are stronger than others. Jesus tells us this by saying very clearly that this kind is different, maybe even has a stronger hold on us, and it takes a special spiritual weapon to conquer this kind, and *that weapon is prayer and fasting combined*.

Second, Jesus tells us in His statement that *"nothing is impossible for us."* I did not believe this until I started to see the benefits of prayer and fasting in my own life. Now

I am a believer, and once I totally surrendered and trusted in Jesus and His words, my spiritual life improved considerably, and the quality of my prayer and fasting improved with each and every day.

As we look at fasting as a spiritual weapon, let's first and foremost comprehend that Jesus thought it was so important that He taught it to the disciples to be used as a special deterrent against evil. These are the same evils that plague our world today: the attack on life, the attack on the family, the attack on our religious freedoms, and the attack on Christianity as a whole. It's especially important to recognize that our actions and our participation can change all of this evil. This is why we are being told by Jesus that "*nothing is impossible for us.*"

This message is loud and clear when we read Pope Emeritus Benedict's Lenten message of 2009 when he says, "this practice (fasting) needs to be rediscovered and encouraged again in our day." He also says that "it seems abundantly clear that fasting represents an important ascetical practice, a spiritual arm to do battle against every possible disordered attachment to ourselves."

Fasting can break the hold of sin and can eliminate the vices and addictions that are keeping us from becoming a faith-filled child of God. I pointed this out in Chapter Four of my book, *From the Hub to the Heart.* Sin had a deep hold on me and something had to give. I had never really said that I wanted to stop drinking, swearing and lying. But when I fasted, it caused a renewal of my soul. Prayer and fasting helped me to overcome all the impure thoughts, the vulgar mouth with which I swore 1500 times a day, the disrespect and pre-judging of all mankind, the excessive drinking, the prideful talk and the lying to everyone about who I was. Gradually, all of those vices were taken away; not by me, but by an almighty and merciful God who had plans for me to work on His team. I cannot explain it, but it all worked out as long as I said "Yes" to fasting. God took care of everything else.

It goes way beyond what we might think or say because it's a grace from God. Fasting can purify our actions and thoughts, can be an inner healer, and certainly gives more power over the cravings of the flesh. I accomplished this only by combining prayer and fasting along with the Sacrament of Confession. This all kept me on the correct spiritual path.

There are over 42 references to fasting in the Old Testament alone. In Saint Matthews's Gospel, Chapter 5, this is where I trust that Jesus is putting the solution right in front of us when he says "*When* you fast."

When I am speaking about fasting during talks around the country, I use this Scripture verse to make the point that Jesus is not saying *if* we consider fasting. Jesus picks His words very carefully. The word 'when' is very important here. 'When' implies that we are doing the action or at least *should be* doing it. I believe that Jesus is telling us that fasting is just as important today as it was thousands of years ago.

From the experiences I will share throughout this book, fasting is a discipline and practice that, when accomplished regularly with prayer, can change lives and make what may seem as the impossible *very* possible with Jesus.

I believe Saint Matthews's Gospel is rich with references to fasting, so this is where Jesus emphasizes that prayer and fasting go together. How? He does so in the Scripture reading in which Jesus gives us the great gift of teaching us how to pray, the Lord's Prayer: "Our Father, who art in heaven."

So praying with and to Jesus is very important, but what does fasting have to do with it? A few sentences after He gives the gift of prayer, Jesus gives us the importance of the discipline of fasting. When we combine these two virtues — prayer and fasting — we are saying to the world that nothing can or will stand between us and Jesus. We are not running towards more food, or money, or alcohol, or anything that is a worldly desire. Our focus is on putting Jesus first, and we are willing to sacrifice things of the world to elevate this focus.

Prayer and fasting will change you, but I also like to fast for the benefit and gifts we can give to others. Prayer and fasting can be used for us *and* for the spiritual benefit of those we love and for those we don't even know.

One last thought on why prayer and fasting should be used together comes from Saint Peter Chrysologus: "Fasting is the soul of prayer, mercy is the lifeblood of fasting. Let no one try to separate them, they cannot be separated. Follow these teachings if you want peace in your life."

With all the biblical references and teachings from Jesus about fasting, I believe that all Christians — regardless of status — are called to fast.

The most important reason we should fast is that Jesus Himself fasted before every major life event. He thought fasting was so important that He taught it. Our Lord spent 40 days in the desert preparing for His ministry by fasting day and night. He was led by the spirit into the desert and was tempted by the evil one. Jesus soundly defeated the devil while in the desert and showed us *the tool to defeat evil is fasting.* Fasting provides a dynamic strength, and it's that strength that God almighty gives us to win and defeat evil in our world. Most importantly, *it's our participation that can defeat this evil.*

Just like with all the Scripture, parables, and lessons that Jesus taught, He did so for our benefit, to use the lessons in this life and to help us get to heaven. So I beg you to try this discipline. Ask yourself: am I prepared for any important events that are coming up in my own life?

Once you surrender and commit, be ready to see Our Lord totally change your life, because He has radically changed mine.

Questions

1. Do you not think that when God Almighty created our complex bodies and then gave us the command of "when you fast" that he would not design the strength and graces necessary for us to accomplish His command to fast?

2. What worldly attractions are keeping us from at least trying this discipline of fasting?

3. What sacraments combined with spiritual tools might be useful in helping me to succeed at fasting?

Chapter Two

The State of Evil in Our World

"The people of Nineveh believe God; they proclaimed a fast and all of them, great and small, put on sackcloth...when God saw by their actions how they turned from their evil way, he repented of the evil he had threatened to do to them; he did not carry it out." (Jonah 3 5-10)

Up until the 1960s, fasting was important and crucial in the life of most Catholics. During Lent, Catholics were obliged to fast most of the 40 days. Once the Lenten obligation to fast was decreased to only two days, fasting was no longer seen as very important.

It is no accident or coincidence that the unimportance of fasting in our world has given Satan and his demons an opening to create more evil every day. Fasting is a lost discipline rarely practiced and not often taught.

Of course, the evil one has already convinced many that he does not exist. Maybe we are too active and too busy in our own lives to recognize the evil one and the violence he brings.

The power of darkness *does* exist, and he and his army of demons will prevail and keep causing fear in us until we get off the bench and join the fight. Jesus has already shown us how to win this fight.

Our Lady of Kibeho has said, "The world is on the edge of catastrophe. To avoid this, the whole world is invited to pray and fast."

Our Lady has told us this fight against evil is one we must start paying attention to. The Mother of God is also *our* mother, and she has been pleading with us for hundreds of years to fight evil through her endorsement of prayer and fasting.

Examples of Evil

This is the 21st century. In our current culture, our lives are filled with forms of witchcraft, freemasonry, generational curses, and sin that have been passed down from past generations and are continuing to threaten generations to come. Our governments and those around the world are removing God and His commandments from society, our schools, and our neighborhoods by establishing immoral laws regarding abortion, gay marriage, and now even transgender rights. We are a world divided and God is nowhere to be seen!

Radical Islamic terrorists have all but wiped out Christianity in the Middle East.

Even worse, many of us are sitting back and doing nothing about it.

There has been an increase in satanic black masses that are defacing Our Lord in the Holy Eucharist for the purpose of mocking God and worshiping the devil. Some of the media, our film industry, many artists, musicians, and magicians are embracing evil in their work, in their writing, in their films, and it's hard to watch anything on TV today.

Recently at Holy Mass, I was distributing Communion, when a lady put the Sacred Host in her pocket. I stopped everything I was doing and walked over to her and asked that she consume the Holy Eucharist. My job as a Eucharistic minister is to protect Our Lord. This is essentially each of our obligations.

The 20th century saw horrible and tragic events, world wars and the Holocaust, the rise of Hitler and other demonic leaders which were responsible for the murders of millions of innocent people. Continuing into this century, there have been plagues and slavery against the people of the world.

We will never forget the attack on the World Trade Center on our own soil killing over 3000 people. Many are afraid to point out that through the sin of abortion, we are suffering a World Trade Center tragedy *each day*. 3000 babies in their mother's womb are murdered *each day* in the name of choice, and few secular media organizations are reporting or talking about this daily heartbreak.

Terrorism Attacks

On December 11, 2016, Egyptian security forces were called to a bombing site that killed over 25 people, mostly women and children. Another 65 were injured during the prayer service. The location was Saint Mark's Cathedral inside St. Peter and St. Paul Coptic Orthodox Church in Cairo. The Islamic State, also known as ISIS, claimed it sent a suicide bomber to the chapel grounds because it had been a known gathering place for Christians to pray.

According to news sources, Pope Francis has declared slain French priest Father Jacques Hamel to be a Christian "martyr," while also condemning murder "in God's name" to be the work of Satan. About Fr. Hamel, the Pope went on to say "this good, humble man, who was always trying to make peace, was assassinated on July 26th, 2016 as if he were a criminal, during the celebration of Holy Mass."

Evil *does* exist and it probably already has affected you

and your family. Some might say, "I know evil is in other parts of the world but will not come to the USA." Some might say, "I really do not believe in these kinds of things."

This is a battle against evil spirits, so who possibly could be responsible for all this violence? In the Paris terrorist attacks in 2015 as the crowd was out partying in a nightclub, they were singing a song just before the gunfire opened up to kill over 100 people and wounding hundreds of others. The name of the song? *Kiss the Devil*.

We must start taking these events very seriously because they are having a major influence in our lives and throughout the world. This evil continues to destroy our families, our society, and, yes, has already infiltrated our Church. It's time we join in the fight, not with violence but with peaceful prayer and fasting.

The good news is that wherever Mary, the Mother of God, is, the battle continues and is not forgotten. In Saint Louis De Monfort's book, *True Devotion to the Blessed Virgin*, he says, "that the Virgin Mary will protect us from the evil one, and they both cannot, and will not, ever be in the same place at the same time." So always stay close to Our Lady!

The influences of darkness fear three very influential powers: the Blessed Mother, the Holy Eucharist, and the Word of God. These are serious times and a call for extreme actions of Penance and renunciation of sin and evil through prayer and fasting.

In Father Slavko's book, *Fast with the Heart*, he recalls a conversation with an exorcist priest, Monsignor Milingo, who said "Our Lady performed the first exorcism after original sin when she was presented by God the Father as the new Eve. As I read this, I look to Scripture in Genesis 3: 14. Then the Lord said to the snake "*because you have done this, I will put enmity between you and the Woman, and between your offspring and hers: They will strike at your head.*"

The words of God the Father tell us that enmity means hostility and separation. When he says 'the woman,' He is referring to the Blessed Virgin Mary.

So why is this Scripture verse so important? He uses the word 'offspring.' He is saying that there are two camps: the offspring of Satan and those of his Blessed Mother. His Mother's offspring will strike at your head. Our connection to Our Lady as her offspring guarantees her heavenly role in our salvation and why she is pleading with us to pray and fast.

Ever since the Garden of Eden, Satan has been trying to influence us and tempt us to sin, and the tools of prayer and fasting are given to us by Jesus to fight Satan and all his temptations. So why not just follow the words in that old Nike commercial? Just do it!

Questions

1. How has evil affected your life or your family?

2. As illustrated in Scripture, prayer and fasting were effective in past years. Do you think that in our culture today prayer and fasting can defeat evil in our world?

Chapter 3

What Would Jesus Do?

*"I turned to the Lord God, to seek help,
in prayer and petition, with fasting, sackcloth, and ashes."*
(Daniel 9:3)

A few years ago during Lent, Cardinal Dolan of New York was interviewed by a reporter. The reporter asked him this question: "What historic figure has had an immense impact on your life?" Cardinal Dolan paused and then answered the question by saying, "Of course, Jesus Christ."

The reporter then said, "Cardinal Dolan, I mean a living person, not someone who is dead."

So the cardinal paused for a few seconds, and then looked directly into the reporter's eyes and said, "It's still Jesus Christ, and, yes, He is alive in each of us."

I love this story. For those who believe in Jesus Christ, it reiterates that He is still alive and in charge of all things within the world He created.

In my office at work, there is a framed picture on the wall of Saint Peter sinking in the storm-filled sea as he attempts to walk on the water to meet Jesus. Peter has certainly lost his focus on Jesus and is concentrating his thoughts on the roaring waters.

When we do this as human beings, we focus on the problem and not the solution. The picture shows Jesus firmly on the water like a linebacker in a defensive stance ready to pounce on the quarterback. Jesus is then reaching out to save a sinking Peter. My thought each day as I look at this picture is that it's clear to me that Jesus is always reaching for us, no matter how much we doubt or mistrust Him. The real question here is, are we reaching for Him?

Each day, I try to trust in His plan and not mine.

This reminds me of a great homily given by Father Peter Grover at Saint Clement's in Boston. He described his own death and judgment. While at the Gates of Heaven, he told the gatekeeper that he was a priest. That was not enough to get into heaven, and that surprised him. Fr. Grover said, "I want you to know that when God the Father asked me to be a priest, I trusted in all He had in store for me." The gatekeeper of heaven said, "Trust. That's what I was looking for to get you into eternity. Come on in."

I tell these stories to paint the picture of Jesus being alive today through all things, and even though some of us — like Peter — doubt and fall deep into the surging waters, Jesus is alive and here to save us. This is why He was born on Christmas Day in Bethlehem thousands of years ago. He came to save us and show us examples by His own life how to live our lives. When we have Jesus in our lives, there is only life, life here on earth and life in eternity.

One more story. I was in my car during Advent last year when a reporter was on the radio interviewing a priest. The reporter was telling the story about Catholic mangers without the Christ Child. The priest told the reporter that most Catholics only put the baby Jesus in the crib when Christmas Day arrives. Then the priest said, "Many people come by before Christmas and look and say that something is missing here." Yes, that is exactly the point! If Jesus is missing from your life, you might want to reexamine how you are living your life.

Just as Cardinal Dolan points out, Jesus is alive today. This is no mistake; the fact is, Jesus is alive in each of us, whether you believe it or not. I receive His precious Body and Blood daily through the hands of the priest during Holy Mass. Jesus is alive through the words of Scripture that we read and are taught each day. The written word of Scripture is alive by our actions, and Our Lord is depending on us to live it out.

As mentioned in the last chapter, evil is present in our world. So I believe that Jesus is telling us to go to the next level and not just pray — but pray *and* fast. And not just during Lent.

Jesus is saying that there is no substitute for fasting. I can tell you in my own life that fasting goes beyond just the refusal of food but fasting also filters into your actions and your thoughts. Fasting taught me a lot about myself, my addictions, cravings, desires — which mostly lead to sin — and I quickly learned by fasting what was essential and non-essential in my life. I also learned that prayer and fasting as a team are critical to bringing about change in my life. Even in serious situations, it's like a total reset button — a new beginning. Like Scripture says, "new wineskins," *out with the old and in with the new*. I believe Jesus is telling us that prayer and fasting are critical to bringing about widespread spiritual change in our world today.

So why aren't more people fasting today? The answer is that it's not easy. What good things can we ever achieve that are really easy? We tend to fall right into the temptation of the evil one, and we are all weak. Our flesh controls our bodies.

If you learn anything from this book, it's that fasting makes us stronger, not weaker. Prayer and fasting are a team and cannot be separated. Proper fasting results in freedom, detachment from vices, a spiritual conversion, and a dynamic spiritual strength, that give us a clear and better understanding of God's will for our lives. For me, fasting gets rid of all the garbage and distractions and creates inner peace.

Most trainers at the gym and professional nutritionists tell us that three full meals per day with snacks in between are what we need. These people may be smart, but they did not make our bodies. God the Father did, and we should listen to Him.

Let me illustrate this with the biblical story of the Transfiguration. A voice comes from the sky and says, *"This is my beloved Son, in whom I am well pleased. Listen to him."* Fasting is one of those things I learned by trying it, and now I can tell you it's time to listen to God. I have confidence and experience that if you removed fasting from our lives, that would take away an opportunity to grow in holiness and come closer to Jesus.

So how does Jesus want us to fix the problems of the world and the problems of our lives?

This is how: If all of us — priests, bishops, cardinals, and pastors of other faiths, along with all the laity — were united in prayer and fasting, we could bring down the barriers that isolate us. Christ works miracles when we pray *and* fast. That can be done under the one discipline, that is, to renew fasting in all of our lives. If all of us were to fast, the world would be a place of peace and tranquility.

We can just look at September 2013, the world was on the verge of a full-scale war in Syria. Pope Francis was new to the world scene and boldly proclaimed a day of prayer and fasting for peace in the world during his Wednesday Angelus talk. It's not the proclamation, but what he said that was important.

"Today, dear brothers and sisters, I wish to add my voice to the cry which rises up with increasing anguish from every part of the world, from every people, from the heart of each person, from the one great family which is humanity: it is the cry for peace! It is a cry which declares with force: we want a peaceful world, we want to be men and women of peace, and we want in our society, torn apart by divisions and conflict, that peace break out! War never again! Never again war! Peace is a precious gift, which must be promoted and protected.

To this end, brothers and sisters, I have decided to proclaim for the whole Church on 7 September next, the vigil of the birth of Mary, Queen of Peace, a day of fasting and prayer for peace in Syria, the Middle East, and throughout the world, and I also invite each person, including our fellow Christians, followers of other religions and all men of good will, to participate, in whatever way they can, in this initiative.

Let us ask Mary to help us to respond to violence: Help us, Mary, to overcome this most difficult moment and to dedicate ourselves each day to building in every situation an authentic culture of encounter and peace. Mary, Queen of Peace, pray for us!"

There are some very important points in his message. First, he is asking all of us to participate, "*all men of good will*," to pray and fast for this cause. Next, he is asking the Mother of God to intercede.

Our Lady, through her numerous apparitions, is calling on us to pray and fast. If we follow her request, we know that, in our own heart and soul, we have done all we can to follow the Queen of Peace. We trusted in her Son, and we fasted like Him.

Questions

1. We are all called to imitate Jesus. What disciplines did Jesus practice that we could also practice to defeat evil in our world today?

2. Throughout this book, it is emphasized that prayer should be used together with fasting. Why do you think prayer and fasting as a team are so important to our spiritual life?

3. Do your family and friends know who you are based on your actions and demeanor?

Chapter Four

Virtues to Fight:
Spiritual Warfare

"Jesus himself has shown us by his own example that prayer and fasting are the first and most effective weapons against the forces of evil." John Paul II, Evangelium Vitae (1994)

"But Jesus took him by the hand, raised him, and he stood up. When he entered the house, his disciples asked him in private, "Why could we not drive it (the demon) out?" He said to them, "This kind can only come out through prayer and fasting." (Mk 9: 27-29)

Precision, accuracy, and authority mean everything in spiritual warfare. This is why fasting is necessary today. Fasting is a virtue and a form of penance that we need to fight the spiritual battle. Since fasting invites the Holy Spirit into our hearts, the reward is increased virtue. Lack of virtue is a sign of lack of self-control. Lack of self-control is a major factor to losing any spiritual battle.

In the fall of 2016, the *Live the Fast* staff was invited to a retreat with exorcist and priest, Father Chad Ripperger. His goal was to teach us more about the discipline of fasting. Some of the content in this chapter is from our time spent with him on retreat, and our time together that proved to be very valuable as we continue moving forward to promote prayer and fasting.

One of the first things Father Ripperger told us was that he fasted six days per week. When I asked why six days, he responded that during an exorcism, the demon will not recognize the exorcist's authority unless he is completely connected to Jesus Christ. Fasting six days a week gives him this grace. This made total sense because it ties in to the temptation of the demon.

The regular everyday person is not involved with exorcism but is being tempted many times a day. Fasting as a spiritual habit and discipline provides authority over the temptation and shows that *you're* in charge and *not* the demon and his temptation. In Father Ripperger's case of fighting the demonic, fasting is necessary for his vocation, but it is also an essential tool for us in the fight against evil. Fasting — along with prayer — is a combined discipline that increases the level of spirituality and brings more needed virtue to each person's life.

The habit of regular fasting becomes a virtues skill and puts all things in the natural order just as God the Father intended. Fortitude, temperance, and a strong will increase with fasting and then provide virtue to calm down the brain waves that clearly need a breakthrough to provide right order. A proper fasting habit creates all things to be subordinate, and then places the mind and body in right order. Right order is our action which only under our control, aligned with God's will, through the direction of the Holy Spirit, is the criteria for everything that we do. Right order leads us to virtue, goodness, peace and only what God the Father desires for us. We cannot reach sainthood without virtue, and a body well-versed in fasting becomes one of increased virtues.

Moving towards the flesh and the body, this is where the desire for repeated bad habits, addictions and vices come from. Most people believe that, without food, they will starve or even die. This is because of the link between the stomach and the brain. The five senses are turned off by fasting because they see food as pleasing and the stomach communicates this to the brain. The imagination works by creating pictures that are pleasing to the flesh and brain.

My ultimate meal is pepperoni pizza, well done, crispy, with a glass of milk. How is that for a visual image?

The body takes delight in food and sexual pleasure. When food becomes gluttony and sexual pleasure becomes lust, these two vices can be broken by the practice of fasting. I have been able to break many other bad habits because of fasting, but these are only two of them. Fasting becomes an entirely new experience for the body, after which, done properly, then becomes pleasing to the brain. So now it wants to repeat the new skill. When the body fasts, it starts to realize the truth about fasting. Its desire for food and pleasure is broken and then it recognizes fasting as a virtue, and it's pleasing to the body and to the mind. Like anything else, fasting becomes easier the more we practice it. The body then will adjust itself.

A human body can live for days, even weeks on just water. As we fast, we will be able to spiritually protect those under our responsibility through the virtue of fasting. I have said this before, but fasting is one of the few things that we can do for ourselves and for the benefit of those we love. This is why Jesus taught fasting. Practiced regularly and learned by the body He created for us, fasting can provide right order and significant spiritual progress. Fasting always brings me closer to God.

Father Ripperger made the point that Jesus shows us there is an obligation to fast as a matter of justice and charity, but fasting is especially important to all those in leadership positions.

Once I started to fast, my decision-making process

became much clearer. If you're in management and have control over decisions that affect people's lives, let me make this point. Priests, pastors, parents, and most people in authority are very comfortable in their life and are unwilling to fast. This action or pride becomes a field that the demon loves to play in. Perception causes emotion, and emotion causes disorder, and it's exactly this disorder where the demon lives. We can all prevent this condition with regular fasting and prayer.

Demons

The demons' plan is simply to disrupt our lives and pull us away from God. Demons have access to all our intellect, and also to our imagination, and will always make things look better than they are, and that will drastically affect our judgment. Their primary job is to influence our intellect and decision by providing pictures and images that cause emotion that affect our overall judgment, to create disorder and divide our lives and put things in shambles that we just give up. One thing the demon loves to do is use other people against us, even the ones closest to us, our spouses, brothers, sisters, children, friends, or just anyone who is weak and gives an opening to the influence of the demon.

The attacks of the demon will come in four distinctive ways and may prevent us from concentration on our prayer life. These are: distraction, dryness, lack of faith and — the favorite of the evil one — discouragement.

As we look at these four schemes, let us first address distractions. What I found to be effective is my willingness to pray and persevere. If that does not work for me, I always ask God for help.

For me, dryness is usually a result of a worldly attachment trying to get me to stop or to quit. The second option is to forget my feelings or worldly attachments and focus on Our Lady and her trust and hope in her Son.

Then there is lack of faith. It takes a genuine focus on Our Lord as the gift giver, and His enormous unending love for me that will keep me from having a lack of faith.

Discouragement can be a combination of the first three, but it's really a matter of not trusting in God, regardless of the results. My lack of trust usually results in me telling God what I would do with this situation instead of just listening and trusting in Him. Most of these tactics are all results of material and worldly things. Fasting elevates prayer and aids me in placing the emphasis on the spiritual and not the worldly. The better I become at fasting, the more profound my prayer life is, and the more I pray, the better I fast.

One last very important point: *all demons are afraid of those who fast*. This is because with prayer and fasting in our lives, he knows his temptations will fail, and he hates that.

"Be not afraid."

Do not be afraid or discouraged and give up, because now we have a weapon to use against Satan's evil plan. The more we stand and fight with prayer and fasting, the more the evil one will be afraid of us. Fasting creates excellence in spiritual virtue by purification, and it becomes a supernatural virtue that is pleasing to God and our penances for our sins are preparation for eternity. We must remember that Jesus Himself fasted to defeat the demons, and all temptations, and if we follow His example, we can do just as He did.

Here are other tools Father Ripperger recommended against the demonic:

1. Consecrate all things to Our Lady and *be specific*. All things are family, friends, work, all tasks, and projects.

2. Pray before every encounter.

3. Pray the Seven Sorrows Devotion and the Rosary, and ask Our Lady to reveal what is keeping the person you're praying for from her Son, Jesus. This will protect your family. Our Lady, through this devotion, will reveal things to you as a way of grace.

4. Pray the binding prayer below. All demons are afraid of any authority or command in Jesus' name.

In the name of the Lord Jesus Christ of Nazareth, by the power of His cross, His blood and His resurrection, I bind you Satan, the spirits, powers and forces of darkness, the nether world, and the evil forces of nature.

I take authority over all curses, hexes, demonic activity and spells directed against me, my relationships, ministry endeavors, finances, and the work of my hands; and I break them by the power and authority of the risen Lord Jesus Christ. I stand with the power of the Lord God Almighty to bind all demonic interaction, interplay and communications between spirits sent against me, and send them directly to Jesus Christ for Him to deal with as He wills.

I ask forgiveness for and renounce all negative inner vows that I have made with the enemy, and ask that Jesus Christ release me from these vows and from any bondage they may have held in me. I claim the shed blood of Jesus Christ, the Son of the living God, over every aspect of my life for my protection. Amen.

5. Have Masses said for your intention or for a person while they are alive.

6. Pray and fast for the person in question.

Questions

1. Do I have a clear understanding of how my mind and body work? But especially how the pictures in my mind and the sins of the flesh can keep me from fasting?

2. When you are discouraged and want to give up, are you energized, impacted by the prayers of others that are fasting along with you?

3. Has this chapter given you a better understanding of why many of us are weak and do not attempt to fast?

Chapter Five

Lent: Ideal Time to Start Fasting

He fasted for forty days and forty nights,
and afterwards he was hungry. (Mt 4,1-2)

Pope Benedict XVI in his 2009 Lenten message said, "At the beginning of Lent, which constitutes an itinerary of more intense spiritual training, the Liturgy sets before us again three penitential practices that are very dear to the biblical and Christian tradition – prayer, almsgiving, fasting – to prepare us to better celebrate Easter and thus experience God's power that, as we shall hear in the Paschal Vigil, "dispels all evil, washes guilt away, restores lost innocence, brings mourners joy, casts out hatred, brings us peace and humbles earthly pride" *(Paschal Præconium).*"

Lent is a time of preparation, a time of spiritual renewal, a time of "more intense spiritual training." It is a time when we join with other Catholics to focus on prayer, almsgiving and fasting.

Why, then, do we look at fasting as a punishment as opposed to a gift? *"But Jesus took him by the hand and lifted him to his feet, and he stood up. After Jesus had gone indoors, his disciples asked him privately, 'Why couldn't we drive it (demon) out?' He replied, 'This kind can come out only by prayer and fasting.'"* (Mark 9:27-29) Fasting has power to cast out demons! Fasting *is* a gift. It is time to ramp up the fight against evil. Jesus has taught us by His example. If we could live these Lenten practices each day throughout the year, what a world it would be. It's participation by us, along with the Sacraments, combined with renunciation that will defeat these evils.

But are we willing to sacrifice? Are we willing to change?

The 21st century is a time of advancements in technology. But it is also a time of distractions. We are distracted by cell phones, TV, social media, news outlets, video games, sports, emails, and our daily schedule. We are so involved and so busy with things of this life that we really do not have time for anything else. *Silence is a weapon against all these distractions*. We cannot have a solid prayer life without being silent and meditating on our prayer.

The practice of prayer and fasting is not 'all or nothing.' How can I make time to go to Mass at least weekly? How can I pray? How can I change? Stepping away for an hour or longer and turning to God is a recipe for how to start. I do it now in Adoration or in morning prayer; that's my silent time with Our Lord. Prayer and fasting are a great way to start and Lent is a good time to get committed since so many others are fasting.

The Church has specific times in the year when we must do penance and be aware of all God's graces in our life. Those two seasons are Lent and Advent. In Lent we prepare for 40 days, starting on Ash Wednesday right up to Triduum by looking at ourselves the way God might look to us. Ash Wednesday is one of the most significant days in the yearly calendar and it's the beginning of a time of repentance. It's a time of spirited effort to turn away from our every day lives by using the three pillars of Lent: prayer, fasting, and almsgiving. It is my hope and prayer that you will embrace these three pillars for a longer time than just Lent. The benefits of these penances are impactful both in and out of the Lenten season. In fact, I believe they are part of God's law for an ordered life here on earth. For this all to work, we must restore right order and return to our creator. *'Before I formed you in the womb I knew you; before you came to birth I consecrated you; I appointed you as prophet of all nations."*

God knew us when He formed us in our mothers' wombs. He *consecrated* us. Can we really be that person God is asking of us? The gap between what I can accomplish on my own and what I can do with God's help is closed considerably when we join our efforts with God's will and grace.

There is a lot of information out there on fasting and Lent. There are many confusing questions. Who should fast? What are the rules to fast? Should I abstain or fast, and what is the difference? Then the famous Lenten question, 'What are you giving up?' If it seems too confusing, then we won't even try it. But that's how the evil one works: through doubt and confusion.

Why is all this necessary? Our Lord would like all of us to share in this effort to sacrifice and bring more souls to Him. If we are all brothers and sisters, why not support and serve each other? One of the sacrifices we choose to practice during Lent is to fast. Fasting in Lent is a great time to start, and it can certainly strengthen your ability to fast throughout the year.

Sixty years ago, the Church obliged her members to fast each day of Lent. We had one meal a day for 40 days. No fasting on Sunday — which was and is considered a feast day, to recognize the resurrection of Jesus. The graces from this fast were unbelievable; many prayers were answered.

It is said that to break a bad habit or vice, it takes about three weeks. And to cultivate a good habit or virtue, it takes another three weeks. That's the six weeks of Lent right there. We no longer have this lengthy time to get rid of vices and cultivate virtues.

Why did Jesus fast in the desert from earthly food for 40 days? I think the answers are clear. He sought more strength through fasting, and He wanted to center on His father and His plan, in His ministry, His passion, and His resurrection.

My own liberation and surrender started with fasting and my refusal of the flesh. Lent is a time I call upon God the Father for his help. I ask Him through prayer and fasting to take away the sins of sloth, lust, power, pride, idleness, and many others. I ask Him to replace those vices with virtues.

I really never said that I wanted to stop drinking, swearing and lying, but when I fasted, it caused a renewal of my soul. Prayer and fasting helped me to overcome all the impure thoughts, the vulgar mouth with which I swore 1500 times a day, the disrespect and pre-judging of all mankind, the excessive drinking, the prideful talk and the lying to everyone about who I was. Gradually it all was taken away, not by me, but by an Almighty and Merciful God who had plans for me. I cannot explain it, but it all worked out as long as I said "Yes" to fasting. God took care of the rest.

Father Alexander Schmemann was a priest, teacher, and author, and at the time of his death in 1983, he was dean of the teaching seminary in New York. In his book, *Great Lent*, he outlines Lent and its chief purpose. He says that man will always follow his desire; the only question is, are we following the right thing or the wrong desire?

Only you can answer that, but I believe it will take much meditating and thought to make real change. "Our culture," Schmemann says, "is built on the assumption that man can achieve anything by himself."[1]

Up until recently, I believed this to be true. I believed I could achieve anything by myself. Now in my sixties, I know that I cannot achieve anything at all without Jesus by my side. It just cannot be done without Him.

Now it's time to combine our efforts with God's will and restore our love for the Creator, the love that was broken by our sin but reconciled by Our Lord's mercy and forgiveness.

Schmemann then says, "The Lenten season is meant to kindle a 'bright sadness' within our hearts. Its aim is precisely the remembrance of Christ, a longing for a relationship with God that has been lost. Lent offers the time and place for recovery of this relationship. The darkness of Lent allows the flame of the Holy Spirit to burn within our hearts until we are led to the brilliance of the Resurrection."[2]

This relationship he speaks of is one of deeper meaning when we stay on the right path by prayer and fasting. Physical hunger can really teach us something. For me when this occurs, it's a time to realize that I am on the right path, and it's time to pray. The hunger is voluntary and prayerful, but what is central is to realize the message God is sending me.

Simplify your Lent by first following Our Lady's call to fast on bread and water. This is the recipe to grow closer to God. "During the season of Lent," Pope Francis said on Ash Wednesday, 2016, "the Church issues two important invitations: to have a greater awareness of the redemptive work of Christ; and to live out one's baptism with deeper commitment. Follow Joel in Chapter 2 of

Scripture when he says 'return to me with your whole heart, with fasting, weeping, and mourning. Rend your hearts, not your garments, and return to the LORD, your God, for he is gracious and merciful, slow to anger, abounding in steadfast love, and relenting in punishment.'"

I knew it was time I came back to Him by way of His Mother. I could have stayed on the path to destruction, but decided to follow Jesus. What about you?

When I speak about fasting in parishes and conferences, the most common question I get is what is the most important aspect about fasting? I regularly answer by saying to 'just start.' Just start fasting, and Lent is a great time, and then watch all the graces our Lord has in store for those who love him.

Questions

1. Have you ever thought of why you are living in this time and place?

2. What does God want from me in my life in this time and place?

3. What if we took some of the Lenten practices and do them throughout the year? (How much better would the world be?)

Chapter Six

The Saints on Fasting

While they were worshiping the Lord and fasting, the Holy Spirit said, 'Set apart for me Barnabas and Saul for the work to which I have called them.' Then completing their fasting and prayer, they laid hands on them and sent them off. (Acts 13:2-3)

The holy saints were well aware of the benefits and the fruits of fasting. Throughout their lives, they gave this discipline special attention. The quotes in this chapter will give us their secrets that will bear much fruit for us too, but only if we listen to these holy men and women.

According to Paul Thigpen's book, *A Year with the Saints,* St. Francis de Sales, one of the great spiritual directors of the Church, when asked what kinds of spiritual readings are most profitable, advised that "when we choose material for spiritual reading, we should 'always prefer' the authors 'whose name begins with S.' He meant, of course, the saints."[3]

This is a powerful statement because it brings to life the favorite saint or saint quote into a safekeeping of mentorship for each one of us. Many of us pray to the saints, but we could all use a saintly mentor.

Below, this chapter opens with a quote from Saint John Vianney, who was known for his prayer and fasting, as he frequently used this discipline daily. The last quote is one of my favorites because Pope John Paul II tells us to use the example of Jesus to cast away the evil that is corrupting our lives today. I think Jesus is telling us directly that we can cast out this evil if we elevate our spiritual lives.

If these holy saints were walking the earth today, they might say that we are missing a very important discipline that could bring us to a stronger deeper conversion in our faith. Through each one of these quotes, listen to the saint speaking directly to each of us.

***

Saint John Vianney: To a priest who complained about the indifference of people in his parish, St. John Vianney answered: "You have preached, you have prayed, but have you fasted?"

Saint Basil: "In the spiritual fast, the faster abstains from evil intentions, words and deeds. One who truly fasts, abstains from anger, rage, malice, and vengeance. One who truly fasts, abstains from idle and foul talk, empty rhetoric, slander, condemnation, flattery, lying and all manner of spiteful talk. In a word, a real faster is one who withdraws from all evil…As much as you subtract from the body, so much will you add to the strength of the soul…By fasting, it is possible both to be delivered from future evils, and to enjoy the good things to come. We fell into disease through sin; let us receive healing through repentance, which is not fruitful without fasting."

Saint Peter Chrysologus "Fasting is the soul of prayer; mercy is the lifeblood of fasting. Let no one try to separate them, they cannot be separated. So if you pray, fast; if you fast, show mercy; if you want your petition to be heard, hear the petition of others. If you do not close your ear to others, you open God's ear to yourself."

Saint Gregory: "It is impossible to engage in spiritual conflict without the previous subjugation of the appetite."

Saint John Chrysostom: "Do you fast? Give me proof of it by your works. If you see a poor man, take pity on him. If you see a friend being honored, do not envy him. Do not let only your mouth fast, but also the eye, and the ear, and the feet, and the hands, and all the members of our bodies. Let the hands fast, by being free of avarice. Let the feet fast, by ceasing to run after sin. Let the eyes fast, by disciplining them not to glare at that which is sinful... Let the ear fast... by not listening to evil talk and gossip... Let the mouth fast from the foul words and unjust criticism."

Saint Ignatius of Loyola: "The purpose of this restraint of the appetite is twofold. It is to avoid excess, disorder and temptation, but also to provide an effective way of praying and living sacramentally, with the totality of ourselves, in an outward sign of the inward grace we desire, which is true freedom of heart."

Saint Francis De Sales, Ash Wednesday 1622: "Fasting is a virtue only when it is accompanied by conditions which render it pleasing to God. Thus it happens that it profits some and not others, because it is not undertaken by all in the same manner...we know very well that it is not enough to fast exteriorly if we do not also fast interiorly, and if we do not accompany the fast of the body with that of the spirit."

Saint Francis De Sales: "We must fast with our whole heart, that is to say, willingly, wholeheartedly, universally and entirely. If I recount to you St. Bernard's words regarding fasting, you will know not only why it is instituted but also how it ought to be kept. He says that fasting was instituted by Our Lord as a remedy for our mouth, for our gourmandizing, and for our gluttony. Since sin entered the world through the mouth, the mouth must do penance by being deprived of foods prohibited and forbidden by the Church, abstaining from them for the space of forty days. But this glorious saint adds that, as it is not our mouth alone which has sinned, but also all our other senses, our fast must be general and entire, that is, all the members of our body must fast. For if we have offended God through the eyes, through the ears, through the tongue, and through our other senses, why should we not make them fast as well? And not only must we make the bodily senses fast, but also the soul's powers and passions — yes, even the understanding, the memory, and the will, since we have sinned through both body and spirit."

Saint Mother Teresa: "We need to be emptied before God, so he can fill us. Fasting and renunciation are our part of the job in faith. Praying without self-renunciation is just like stopping halfway. But we can die to sin and then evil no longer has authority over us. Renunciation is dying to sin."

Saint John Chrysostom: "Fasting is the support of our soul: it gives us wings to ascend on high, and to enjoy the highest contemplation! God, like an indulgent father, offers us a cure by fasting."

Saint Basil: "Penance without fasting is useless and vain; by fasting we satisfy God."

Saint Catharine of Sienna: "Without mortifying the taste, it is impossible to preserve innocence, since it was by the indulgence of his appetite that Adam fell."

Saint Augustine: "But now the necessity of habit is sweet to me, and against this sweetness must I fight, lest I be enthralled by it. Thus I carry on a daily war by fasting, constantly bringing my body into subjection...And while health is the reason for our eating and drinking, yet a perilous delight joins itself to them as a handmaid; and indeed, she tries to take precedence in order that I may want to do for her sake what I say I want to do for health's sake....These temptations I daily endeavor to resist and I summon thy right hand to my help and cast my perplexities onto thee."

Saint Faustina Kowalska: "Interior mortifications take the first place, but besides this, we must practice exterior mortifications, strictly determined, so that all can practice them. These are: on three days a week, Wednesday, Friday and Saturday, there will be a strict fast; each Friday, all the sisters – each one in her own cell – will take the discipline for the length of the recitation of Psalm 50, and all will do this at the same time; namely, three o'clock; and this will be offered for dying sinners. During the two great fasts, ember days and vigils, the food will consist of a piece of bread and some water, once a day."

Saint Jerome: "Fasting is not merely a perfect virtue: it is the foundation of all the other virtues; it is sanctification, purity, and prudence – virtues without which no one can see God."

Saint Peter of Ravenna: "Fasting, as we all know, is God's fortress, the camp of Jesus Christ, the rampart of the Holy Ghost, the standard of faith, the mark of charity, and the trophy of holiness."

Saint Leo: "Fasting gives strength against sin, represses evil desires, repels temptation, humbles pride, cools anger, and fosters all the inclinations of a good will, even unto the practice of every virtue."

The Blessed Mother, Our Lady of Medjugorje**: "**One cannot fast without love, nor can one love without fasting in its broadest sense. Prayer is also our answer to God's love. That is why fasting and prayer are inseparable. By fasting without prayer we in fact just revolve around ourselves. Fasting turns all our spiritual forces and powers of the heart, all of our inner being towards God."

Saint Francis de Sales: "If you are able to fast, you will do well to observe some days beyond what are ordered by the Church, for besides the ordinary effect of fasting in raising the mind, subduing the flesh, confirming goodness, and obtaining a heavenly reward, it is also a great matter to be able to control greediness, and to keep the sensual appetites and the whole body subject to the law of the Spirit; and although we may be able to do but little, the enemy nevertheless stands more in awe of those whom he knows can fast. The early Christians selected Wednesday, Friday and Saturday as days of abstinence."

Saint Benedict: "All other virtues become possible through fasting, especially the virtue of chastity."

Saint Thomas More: "The scripture is full of places that prove fasting to be not the invention of man but the institution of God, and to have many more profits than one. And that the fasting of one man may do good unto another, our Saviour showeth himself where he saith that some kind of devils cannot be cast out of one man by another 'without prayer and fasting.'"

Saint Leo the Great: "The prayer of fasting is pleasing to God and frightful to Satan. It contributes to the salvation of others as well as to our own. There is nothing more efficacious than fasting in order to come closer to God."

Saint Alphonsus De Ligouri: "To abandon, for God's sake, all worldly enjoyments, has always been the practice of Holy Souls."

Pope Saint John Paul II: *"*Jesus himself has shown us by his own example that prayer and fasting are the first and most effective weapons against the forces of evil.*"* *Evangelium Vitae (1994)*

These quotes clearly show us that fasting is pleasing to God.

In my research, I also discovered that some saints lived solely on the Holy Eucharist. Blessed Alexandrina de Costa, Servant of God Therese Neumann, St. Catherine of Genoa, St. Joseph of Cupertino and St. Catherine of Siena, are just a few. [4]

We are all called to be saints and we all should *want* to be saints. The biggest obstacle we have is sin, sin created by our flesh and worldly desires and seeking things of this world. In order to fight temptation and engage in spiritual battle, fasting is a must. Let us look to each of these saints and many more for an example of how we can create peace and trust in God, just like many of the saints did in their lives.

Questions

1. Which of these saints' quotes do find most inspiring that encourages you to fast?

2. Which is your favorite saint and how would you aspire to be like him or her?

3. Why do you think the saints were attracted to this discipline of fasting?

Chapter Seven

The Didache

They wept, fasted,
and prayed before the Lord.
(Baruch 1:5)

If there is one spiritual document that outlines and stresses the importance of fasting in the spiritual growth of one's life, it's the *Didache* (*pronounced did-uh-kay*). This text has stood the test of time for thousands of years.

Most scholars place its composition between A.D. 60 and 110. However, one of the top scholars alive, Enrico Mazza, argues very persuasively that the liturgical portions of the document were composed no later than 48 A.D. If he's correct, that means that our oldest liturgical texts pre-date most of the books of the New Testament.[5]

It was then, in the first century, that the Christian community produced what we might call its first "catechism," a book that bears the title, *The Teaching of the Lord to the Gentiles through the Twelve Apostles*, or in Greek, simply the *Didache,* the "teaching."

Since the *Didache* was considered to have originated with the apostles, its authority was absolute throughout the first millennium of the Church. Many of the early Church Fathers quote the document, and some included it as part of the New Testament.

The *Didache* is a text that dates back to the first century and is a handbook for a holy Christian life. According to Dr. Aaron Milavec, the *Didache* defines the way of life using two fundamental definitions.[6]

First, what must be done to be holy, and second, what must be avoided?

For me, fasting undoubtedly falls in both of these categories. I certainly need fasting to grow in holiness and become closer to God in all things. Fasting then takes my prayer and its words and converts it to action. My prayer becomes elevated and creates more awareness through fasting so that I can hear God's promptings through the Holy Spirit.

Fasting helps me to avoid the many things of the world that are holding me back from being a child of God. As I have said before, we are buried under our habits of consumerism, especially here in the USA, and fasting has helped me control the desires of my sinful flesh. To continue to enrich my spiritual life, fasting is necessary.

According to an article entitled *The Time Capsule* written by Mike Aquilina, as the apostles went to their martyrdom, one by one, the flock they left behind saw the only eyewitnesses to Jesus' teachings vanishing. So the *Didache* was written.[7]

The main themes that emerge from this holy book are that fasting and prayer should be done for the sake of one's enemies, that fasting is part of the preparation for Baptism, and that fasting should be practiced on different days than the Jews.

Father Tom Hart has recommended the writings and book by Thomas O'Loughlin on the *Didache*. In his chapter on prayer and fasting, he makes the point that in early Christian living, rhythm and sequence had already been established.[8]

In fact, he states the days of the week were originated in Ireland through Christianity. He further states that three of the days are named from the practice of fasting. Wednesday was called *ceadaoin* which means 'first fast day,' and Friday was called *Aoine* which means 'fast day,' but Thursday was named *Deadaoine* which means 'between two fasts.' So the *Didache* makes it very clear that the days of fasting are significant enough to build a weekly sequence and calendar around them.

Just as I learned in Medjugorje that Our Lady is asking us to fast on Wednesdays and Fridays on only bread and water for 24 hours, her messages are concrete, and aligned to the *Didache*, when she tells us to commemorate her Son's betrayal on Wednesday and His Passion on Friday. So this is a practice that dates back to the Apostles and the Early Church. It's clear when reading the *Didache* that the disciples of Jesus fasted on Wednesdays and Fridays.

Just as the *Didache* stresses the importance of fasting, so also must we, especially now, realize the power of fasting. Our Lady tells us, *"You have forgotten that with prayer and fasting, you can ward off wars, suspend natural laws."* By combining prayer and fasting, we increase the power of our prayers especially when praying for a special or urgent intention. By prayer and fasting, we allow our whole being to participate and offer this sacrifice to God. Fasting becomes an active prayer with our body. We should also fast because we love God and want to be soldiers that offer our bodies in the battle against evil.

The *Didache* is also telling us that prayer and fasting go together and are especially linked to personal prayer while practiced in community. These days, my fasting is more powerful and more effective with a fasting partner or in community. Accepting prayer and fasting as a team to fight spiritual warfare is a concept that dates way back to the early Church Fathers.

According to the United States Catholic Bishops' website, the modern day version of the *Didache*, the *Catechism of the Catholic Church,* was written in 1992 and contains much history and background. The *Catechism of the Catholic Church* originated with a recommendation made at the Extraordinary Synod of Bishops in 1985. In 1986 Pope John Paul II appointed a commission of cardinals and bishops to develop a compendium of Catholic doctrine. In 1989 the commission sent the text to all the bishops of the world for consultation. In 1990 the commission examined and evaluated over 24,000 amendments suggested by the world's bishops. The final draft is considerably different from the one that was circulated in 1989. In 1991 the commission prepared the text for the Holy Father's official approval. On June 25, 1992 Pope John Paul II officially approved the definitive version of the *Catechism of the Catholic Church*. On December 8, 1992 Pope John Paul II promulgated the Catechism with an apostolic constitution.

The *Catechism* consists of 2,865 paragraphs, each of which is numbered. There is an internal cross-referencing system among the paragraphs which makes it simple to find all the passages in the *Catechism* which treat a particular subject. For me, even after entertaining 24,000 amendments, the Catechism is lacking on teaching and references to the very important discipline of fasting. In fact, it often uses abstinence for a substitute term for fasting. Our Church lives on tradition and belief, so all references to the *Didache* show us how the early Church, the apostles, and the Saints, used this tool to advance their own discipline and spiritual well-being.

I believe the lack of information about fasting in the Catechism helps define where we are today. A quick review on the internet shows us that Americans spend fifty billion on weight loss products, and the health club industry says consumers are spending eighty billion a year on gym and health club memberships and activities.[9] That is a total of 130 billion. It's a clear indication of what we see as important.

The truth is, as baptized Christians, we are more concerned with the state of our body than that of our soul. Saint John Vianney said this, *"Oh, my children, how sad it is! Three-quarters of those who are Christians labor for nothing but to satisfy this body, which will soon be buried and corrupted, while they do not give a thought to their poor soul, which must be happy or miserable for all eternity."*

We must not forget that our bodies will die, but our souls will live forever. How we live our worldly life will determine the whereabouts of each individual soul's life in eternity. We all need to prepare for the return of Jesus, whether in judgment or in the final days. This is another great reason to fast.

Now over 2000 years after it was written, the *Didache* is not an out-of-date document, but a modern version of the Catechism, and how we can and should live today. Here is a quote from the *Didache* that can look into the lives and teaching of their first century forebearers: *"Bless those who curse you, and pray for your enemies, and fast for those who persecute you."*

Questions

1. Have you ever heard of the *Didache*?

2. Are you surprised to hear that fasting was so essential in the building of the early Church?

3. What are you doing in your life spiritually to prepare for eternity?

Chapter Eight

What is Fasting?

Yet even now—oracle of the LORD—
return to me with your whole heart, with fasting,
weeping, and mourning. (Joel 2:12)

Fasting is an excellent remedy to eliminate addictions of any kind like alcohol, drugs, gambling, smoking, pornography, and many others.

To support this, let's go back to the first critical fast in the Garden of Eden.

Then God said, "*Let us make human beings in our image, after our likeness. So God created mankind in his image: in the image of God, he created them: male and female he created them. God blessed them and said be fertile and multiply, fill the earth and subdue it.*" (Gen 1:27)

God planned for us to have a long, loving, joyful, and fruitful life. Our lives are different today because our sin makes it that way. Why? Because we are weak. The solution? Fasting, because it makes the flesh stronger, *not* weaker. Everyone needs to practice fasting.

The Lord God gave man this order. "*You are free to eat from any of the trees in the garden, except the tree of knowledge of good and evil. From that tree you shall not eat.*" When I read this passage from Scripture, I have the sentiment that God is saying this is your first fast, your first test. Yes, we yielded and became weak and compromised. We forgot about the evil one and his influence on us. The first big mistake was having a conversation with the evil one. Today when that happens to any of us, let us go right to Saint Michael and pray the Saint Michael prayer, composed by Pope Leo XIII.

St. Michael the Archangel, defend us in battle.
Be our defense against the wickedness and snares of the devil.
May God rebuke him, we humbly pray,
and do thou, O Prince of the heavenly hosts,
by the power of God, thrust into hell Satan,
and all the evil spirits, who prowl about the world
seeking the ruin of souls. Amen.

Sometimes I will also read Scripture, or pray for Our Lady's intercession, and the evil will flee. According to Saint Louis de Montfort, Our Lady and the evil one will not — and cannot — be in the same place at the same time.

Back to the Garden of Eden. "The woman saw that the tree was good for food and pleasing to the eyes and the tree was desirable for gaining wisdom. So she took some of its fruit and ate it; and she also gave some to her husband, who was with her, and he ate it." So we refused God's commandment *not* to eat of the Tree of Knowledge, and our actions changed the state of humanity by making our own selfish decisions more important, by doing what *we* want, not what *God* wants for us.

So what was different in the Garden than what we do today? The women saw the tree was good for food and pleasing to the eye. So she took and ate it and then gave some to her husband. Men, do not blame the women because it's our job is to protect, and that means to spiritually protect. That should be our priority.

Back in Chapter Four, I stated that demons have access to all our intellect, and mostly to our imagination, and will always make things look better than they are, and that will drastically affect our judgment. One thing the demon loves to do is to use other people against us, even the ones closest to us, our spouses, brothers, sisters, children, friends — anyone who might be weak and might give an opening to the influence of the demon.

In the Garden of Eden, the woman was weak, judgment was compromised, and they gave in to the temptation. We have two human beings, husband and wife — we cannot get any closer than that — and they failed the test together. This is no different today than it was thousands of years ago. The world is failing the test.

As we look at the temptation in the Garden of Eden, we can't underestimate the power of evil.

Here is another example from Scripture. *(Jn 13: 26-27)*

So he dipped the morsel and handed it to Judas, son of Simon the Iscariot. After he took the morsel, Satan entered him.

If the evil one was present at the Last Supper, do you think he is afraid of tempting us today? Absolutely not. The best part is that we can defeat evil and prevent this sin by the regular practice of prayer and fasting. Fasting is an entirely different arena and level of spirituality. But it is undefeated!!

As you fast, you will find that temptations may seem stronger than ever. That's because they are. The evil one is afraid of those who fast. It was only when Jesus went into the desert and fasted for 40 days that he was first tempted three times by Satan, so we can most certainly expect the same.

Like Jesus, Satan will tempt your hunger. He used the same strategy by tempting Eve in the Garden, Jesus in the desert, and yes — us today. The only difference is that the evil one can control our food consumption with massive chemical addictions and cravings today. *"If you are the Son of God, command that these stones become loaves of bread."* (Mt. 4:3)

Perhaps it will sound more like, *"If you're really going to fast today, you will still need coffee."* Or maybe *"Just a little peanut butter on your bread won't make a difference. You must be so hungry!"* Thankfully, Jesus overcame this temptation and we too can overcome it and pray His words, "It is written: *'One does not live by bread alone, but by every word that comes forth from the mouth of God.'*" In moments of hunger and temptation, let us turn to the Holy Bible and dine on His Word.

One of the best documents ever written on fasting is a document that was written by Pope Benedict, his 2009 *Lenten Message on Fasting*. The Holy Father says, "I wish to focus my reflections especially on the value and meaning of fasting." Then he said, "Jesus, too, through prayer and fasting, prepared Himself for the mission that lay before Him, marked at the start by a serious battle with the tempter."

Look around at the world today. Does anyone *not* believe we are in a serious battle?

If you believe we are in a serious battle, do you think we could do well by preparing? Before every significant event in biblical history, Christ and/or His disciples fasted. So we are saying they prepared for the battle with a Holy Fast. We could do well by doing the same. Pope Benedict XVI provided his own example with the case with Ezra, who, in preparation for the journey from exile back to the

Promised Land, calls upon the assembled people to fast so that *we might humble ourselves before our God*." (Ezra 8:21). The Almighty heard their prayer and assured them of His favor and protection.

Pope Benedict XVI goes on to say, "The Sacred Scriptures and the entire Christian tradition teach that fasting is a great help to avoid sin and all that leads to it. For this reason, the history of salvation is replete with occasions that invite fasting."

"...a great help to avoid sin and all that leads to it." I can personally relate. The evil one had me at his command. Whenever I got into trouble, it typically first started with a great dinner or excessive drinking with my buddies, maybe a prideful cigar, and then the trouble sprang up. Afterward, I usually asked myself, "How did I get here?" So I really understand what the Holy Father is saying. If you want to avoid trouble, then you must control your flesh and your cravings with fasting.

The Holy Father writes, "Fasting is a practice that is encountered frequently and recommended by the saints of every age. Saint Peter Chrysologus writes: 'Fasting is the soul of prayer; mercy is the lifeblood of fasting. So if you pray, fast; if you fast, show mercy; if you want your petition to be heard, hear the petition of others.'"

If we want our Lord to hear our prayers, then incorporate fasting into them. It will be like flagging an email to Our Lord. Heaven will answer the call.

Pope Benedict XVI then says that "fasting seems to have lost something of its spiritual meaning." Well, it has. Why? Because it's not often practiced; we are way too comfortable, and it's rarely ever taught in any section of our lives today. Not in schools, not in our families, and —

believe it or not — not even in our seminaries.

Today we hear the term abstinence used interchangeably with fasting. I learned quickly there is a big difference. Abstinence is giving up a specific food for a period of time and a term often used in Lent. When Lent comes around, the most common question is, "What are *you* giving up?" The typical answer is something like, "For Lent I am giving up chocolate." Big deal! Jesus was betrayed, scourged, crucified and died for our sins, and we're giving up chocolate? Have you ever seen the scourging scene in *The Passion of the Christ*?

Here is the definition: Fasting is a total emptying of ourselves of food and drink. No coffee, butter, jam, jelly, just plain bread and water. By the way, it's bread for a few great reasons. First, Jesus said, *"I am the Bread of life, whoever comes to me will never hunger, and whoever believes in me will never thirst."* (*John 6:35*) The words hunger and thirst make it clear to me that Jesus is referring to bread and water. The second and most important reason to use bread in fasting is that it relates to the Holy Eucharist. I was educated in the importance of attending daily Mass and craving Jesus in the Eucharist. It always helps when I attend Mass on fasting days.

Let me close this chapter with a few more words from Pope Benedict from his 2009 Lenten message. He says, "It seems abundantly clear that fasting represents an important ascetical practice, a spiritual arm to do battle against every possible disordered attachment to ourselves. Freely chosen detachment from the pleasure of food and other material goods helps the disciple of Christ to control the appetites of nature, weakened by original sin, whose negative effects impact the entire human person."

Pope Benedict says something I have been advocating over the last six years: "This practice (fasting) needs to be rediscovered and encouraged again in our day, especially during the liturgical season of Lent."

Pope Francis opens his apostolic letter, *The Joy of the Gospel*, with "The great danger in today's world, pervaded as it is by consumerism, whenever our interior life becomes caught up in its own interests and concerns, there is no longer room for others, no place for the poor. God's voice is no longer heard. This is exactly where fasting comes into play. It opens our hearts and souls to the word of God and allows us to live a holy and virtuous life."

Change your life through the sacraments and support it by prayer and fasting. If I was able to do it, I know you can too!!

Questions

1. If you haven't yet tried fasting, what is keeping you from doing so?

2. Has this chapter given you a better understanding of where and how to start fasting?

3. Are there any addictions, habits or actions that you'd like to change and can fasting assist you in moving in that direction?

Chapter Nine

Why Bread and Water Fast?
Why Wednesday and Friday?

*All the men of Israel cried to God with great fervor
and humbled themselves with much fasting. (Judith 4:9)*

Fasting is often a word that we hear in preparation for Lent, but do we anticipate this practice with joy? Or dread? Who's already planning their one full meal and two small meals (that can't equal one full meal) for Ash Wednesday?

Why is it that we look at fasting as a punishment as opposed to a gift?

"But Jesus took him by the hand and lifted him to his feet, and he stood up. After Jesus had gone indoors, his disciples asked him privately, 'Why couldn't we drive it (demon) out?' He replied, 'This kind can come out only by prayer and fasting.'" – (Mark 9:27-9:29) Fasting has the power to cast out demons! This is a gift! Jesus is teaching us by His example.

In Monsignor Charles Murphy's book, *The Spirituality of Fasting: Rediscovering a Christian Practice*, the Holy Father at the time, Pope John Paul II, was having dinner with the author on February 22, 1980, and he posed a question in part that leads us to today, "What has happened to fasting and abstinence in the United States? They seem simply to have gone away." I wonder what Pope John Paul was thinking when he presented this question to then rector of the North American College in Rome. Did he see how the Church might dearly *need* fasting? Did he believe the United States could really move from a nation of consumerism to leading the world back to God? We know that Pope Saint John Paul II was well ahead of his time, especially in his culture-changing ideas like World Youth Day and the *Theology of the Body*. Is it possible that in 1980, he planted a seed that the Holy Spirit is now cultivating: for America and the world to come together, and to renew the practice of fasting?

Monsignor Charles Murphy references the teachings of desert fathers in his book. He says, "The desert fathers were convinced that the condition of the body reflects the condition of the soul. If this is the case, I am in big trouble, and I can only pray God gives me the time and grace to correct this situation. An undisciplined body reveals an undisciplined soul."[10]

Monsignor Murphy notes that it's significant that the first deadly sin was gluttony. Since all of us are weighed down by sin and its consequences, fasting is proposed as an instrument to restore friendship with God. Monsignor Charles Murphy writes that in the early Church, "Christians were expected to fast every Wednesday and Friday throughout the year." Wednesday was a day of penance because it was believed to be the day Judas betrayed Our Lord. Friday was the day of the crucifixion and death of Jesus.

The late Father Slavko Barbaric, in an interview with Denis Nolan of Mary TV, along with Sister Emmanuel said, "That the weekly calendar in Irish Gaelic language has a noteworthy importance to fasting, and the days of the week. Wednesday means the 'small fast' or the 'first fast,' Thursday means the 'day between the fast,' and Friday means the 'big fast'."

Fr. Slavko points out that in those days, the Irish

Catholic Church was much stronger than it is today. He also says we must look to Thursday and the Last Supper as the day the Holy Eucharist was created.

This is why we fast on bread and water, to crave the Holy Eucharist and to cleanse ourselves with water. It's a prayer with our body that gives us spiritual *and* physical strength. Fasting on bread and water on Wednesday and Friday prepares us for the true encounter with Christ in the Eucharist. We must also practice the Eucharistic fast one hour before Holy Communion each day to prepare for Jesus, to join His holy body and blood with our immoral flesh and body. On fast days, I want to make room for the graces that God Almighty wants to hand out to those who do penance by prayer and fasting.

Bread and water have always been basic necessities of life. Now, because of the messages of Our Lady of Medjugorje, this type of fasting has become increasingly popular and also a complete devotion. On August 14, 1984, visionary Ivan Dragicevic was told by Our Lady this message: "*I would like them to fast strictly on Wednesday and Friday, and to pray at least the rosary every day, the Joyful, Sorrowful, Glorious mysteries.*"

I'd like to point two things out. First, the 'alleged' apparitions of Medjugorje are still ongoing as of the writing of this book and have yet to be approved by the Church. Second, back in 1984, Pope John Paul II had not yet introduced the Luminous Mysteries of the Holy Rosary.

To help those who want to follow a bread and water fast, *Live the Fast*-approved breads are made with no GMOs (genetically modified organisms), totally clean label, no preservatives or additives, and plenty of nutrition to get through the fast day. It's important to understand that the first part of digestion begins in the mouth, so we should chew the bread slowly to get the full benefit and nutritional value. We must also drink plenty of water and listen to our body when fasting. We recommend that everyone seeks the advice of a spiritual director and/or doctor before beginning a strict fast.

Saints who founded orders such as Saint Benedict, Saint Francis de Sales and Saint Faustina included Wednesday, Friday and Saturday fasting on bread and water in their rules of life. Saturday was in preparation for Resurrection Sunday. "Besides the ordinary effect of fasting in raising the mind, subduing the flesh, confirming goodness, and obtaining a heavenly reward, it is also a great matter to be able to control greediness, and to keep the sensual appetites and the whole body subject to the law of the Spirit."[11]

Father Adalbert De Vogue is an enthusiastic supporter of the Benedict rule of fasting. In his book, *To Love Fasting*, he says, "We must experience fasting and then we will love it. To love fasting, one must experience it, but to experience it, one must love it." This cycle changes, he says, when we trust in God and look at the examples of the saints.[12]

Most of us are uneducated and confused about the discipline of fasting. How do we choose what is right for our bodies and when it is the right time to fast?

Personally, I try to define my vision of what a prayer and fasting habit looks like. Why is it necessary today? Who is encouraging me to do this? It's a matter of who we are and what defines each one of us.

In my experience, it always leads back to the Mother of God. It is our responsibility to follow her messages, her call, and to look back on the Church Fathers and many saints, and see the reason behind their practice of a bread and water fast on Wednesday and Friday. Today we are really looking for a solution. We are looking to create real change. Why not follow Our Lady's message?

In Father Slavko's book, *Fast with the Heart*, he states, "Today by living on bread and water, man retains his freedom. He does not become a slave to material things. In his fasting, man is free to love, free to forgive, and free to live in peace."[13]

Fasting is where real change begins.

Questions

1. What do you think that Pope St. John Paul II was thinking when he asked the question: *What has happened to fasting and abstinence in the United States*?

2. When God the Father created our bodies, did you realize that you could pray with your body by fasting?

3. How does the bread and water fast relate to the Holy Eucharist?

Chapter Ten
Fasting Basics/ Benefits

And then as a widow until she was eighty-four.
She never left the temple, but worshiped night and day
with fasting and prayer. (Luke 2:37)

Preparation for a fast day begins the evening before. Spend time in prayer with Jesus, Our Lord, or the Blessed Mother, seeking the wisdom from the Holy Spirit, to determine the length of the fast you're ready to complete the next day. Fasting should be moved into gradually, so to establish a 12- hour, 18-hour or 24-hour fast will be central to accomplishing your sacrifice. Then ask the Lord to prepare your heart, your mind, and your body for the next day and the fast.

Once you commit yourself to prayer and fasting, the temptations to abandon are going to be strong. As you fast, you will find that these temptations may seem stronger than ever before, and that's because they are. It was only when Jesus went into the desert and fasted for 40 days that he was first tempted three times by Satan. So we can most certainly expect the same, even the identical temptations. Just like Jesus, Satan will tempt your hunger. So prayer and preparation for the upcoming temptations will determine how well you do. Remember that the evil one does not want you to fast, and he is afraid of those who fast. Remember that the Lord's invitation is not only to fast, but to pray. God is calling you to a more profound relationship with Him. Fasting, combined with prayer, is the beginning of real change.

The next morning, on your fast day, your experience will be entirely defined by how you start your day, and it will impact the rest of your day. With this in mind, each and every fast day should begin with prayer. You may pray the fasting prayer that is included in Father Slavko's book, *Fast with the Heart*, or you may pray the Chaplet of the Holy Fast, which you will find at the end of this book.

I recommend that you pray both prayers for strength to follow God's command of "when we fast."

Be sure to relay any thoughts, worries, concerns, or excitements you might have about fasting that day to the Lord Jesus. Call on the Holy Spirit for enlightenment to what graces you need.

Fasting is a gift and a grace given to those who persevere. In the Chaplet of the Holy Fast, the Saint Michael prayer is recited to eliminate any evil distractions or temptations we might have to distract us or to cause us to quit. Thank God for calling you closer to Him through fasting. Thank God for the gift of being His child.

In the fasting prayer, it's important to stay focused on your particular intention and what or who you are fasting for. This task permits you to fight all temptation by realizing the purpose behind your effort at fasting. Take your time when you add your intentions. The more specific they are, the more you'll be grounded in them and find the strength to fast for them later in the day. Perhaps even write them down.

Fasting is one of the few things we can do for the benefit of others and ourselves. Call on the Holy Spirit to fill your heart and mind with intentions. What's heavy on your heart? Who needs healing? Who would you pray for? If you find yourself going through the motions, discouraged or without peace, it is most likely because there's insufficient time spent in prayer. Fasting and prayer go hand in hand; if you pray well, you will fast well.

Fasting Prayer

Father, today I resolve to fast. I choose to fast
because your prophets fasted,
because your Son, Jesus Christ, fasted,
as did His apostles and disciples.

I decide to fast because your servant,
Mother Mary, also fasted.
I fast today as a disciple of your Son
and I ask for the intercession
of the saints and my guardian angel.

Father, I present this day of fasting to you
for the ability to discover Your Word more
and discover what is essential and
non-essential in this life.

I present this fast to you for peace —
for peace in my heart, peace with my family,
peace with my neighbors, peace in my town/city,
state and my country.

I fast for peace in the world, for all troubled spots in the
world.
I remember those who are hungry and impoverished.

I fast today for (your intentions).

Through this fast, cleanse me of all bad habits
and calm down my passions and
let Your virtues increase in me.
Let the depth of my soul open
to Your grace through this fast,
so that it may totally affect and cleanse me.
Father, please help me fast with my heart.

*Mary, you were free in your heart and
bound to nothing except the Father's will.*

*Please obtain by prayer the grace of a joyful fast for me
today.*
Our Father...Hail Mary...Glory Be! Amen.

*Adapted from "Fast with the Heart" fasting prayer by
Father Slavko Barbaric.*[14]

Whether you're an experienced faster, a new faster or a fallen-off-the-wagon-but-trying-again faster (like most of us are), there is a starting point for you.

In most of my fasting talks, the first question people ask is what is the most important part of fasting? The important fact is *that you start*. Just do it. Sound familiar? It's the tagline of the old Nike commercial. Just start fasting and see the graces flow. I promise you!

We come from different walks of life and of faith, which is why some people will be able to jump right into the bread and water fast twice a week, and others may need to start by just eliminating snacks two days a week. The range of "starts" is as numerous as there are individuals. Through prayer and discernment with the Lord, He will guide you on how to start. The Lord knows you, your strengths, your weaknesses, your personality, and He knows the future with as much confidence as He knows the present and the past. Pray to the Holy Spirit for the gift of knowledge. Ask the Lord for His help, that you may better understand yourself and how He is calling you to pray and fast. Remember this: when hunger comes my way, when I am tempted, I look at it as, "I am on the right path, and it's time to pray." Fasting combined with prayer makes us stronger — not weaker.

The key is to start incrementally. Just as one wouldn't go to the gym for the first time and try bench-pressing 250 pounds, the same is true for fasting. Fasting muscles need to be trained, strengthened and stretched. Fasting is a journey and takes time, perseverance and, most importantly, patience. Due to our sinful human nature, there will be times when we fail or feel like we failed. Do not fall into the trap of discouragement! Do not think: "Fasting just isn't for me. I'm not a faster." These deceitful thoughts are harmful and do not come from the Lord. Bring this to Jesus, and He will transform them into hope. Remember that *all fasting is pleasing to the Lord*.

You should always discuss fasting and prayer challenges and celebrations with your parish priest or spiritual director. Also those with medical challenges must consult their doctor before beginning the practice of fasting.

Once you've prayed, and prepared spiritually and mentally, then it's time to bake your bread for the day and enjoy your first roll. In Father Aldabert De Vogue's book, *To Love Fasting*, he recommends eating only eight to ten ounces of bread per 24-hour fast. See the preparation video on our website livethefast.org.

When eating the breads, be sure to take small bites and chew each bite for 45-60 seconds. Digestion begins in the mouth! Drink plenty of water throughout the fast day. The absolute most important scheduling of the day is to attend Holy Mass and receive the precious Body and Blood of Jesus. I do this at noon on fast days. Noon Mass always seems to elevate my prayer and fill my soul with the spiritual nourishment that is required to accomplish the fast. Another powerful practice on fast days is Eucharistic Adoration. The ultimate prayers of Holy Mass together with Adoration are key ways to incorporate both prayer and fasting. Whether you receive Jesus at Mass or pray to Him in Adoration, He is present as the Bread of Life.

So why is a bread man promoting and writing about fasting? Being in the bakery business for more than 40 years, I realized that food manufacturers are inserting chemicals and additives into the vast majority of foods to make consumers crave more and more. Man has manipulated the God-given gifts of wheat and grain, genetically modifying them to make flour tailored for extended shelf-life and increased profits. It is very difficult to fast on these modern-day breads because they will accelerate one's appetite and cause other side effects that are discouraging to the fast. They might look the same or taste the same, but as soon as they get into your stomach, watch out.

Live the Fast-approved breads are all-natural and made with pure ingredients directly from the earth, so your body can consume the highest basic nutrition. Be assured that all wheat used in the production of our fasting breads has NOT been genetically modified. These artisan breads have no artificial preservatives, additives or dough conditioners. They are made according to methods using wholegrain flour, natural bran, 12 grains, cereals and old-world flours. The breads are manufactured in a temperature-controlled environment which ensures the highest nutritional value that will help you to complete your daily tasks so you can *live the fast*. The most important reason behind my efforts to promote prayer and fasting is that it changed my life, and I believe it can change yours. Fasting and prayer make the impossible very possible.

Simply put, fasting in community or with a fasting partner makes fasting less challenging. There are many benefits of doing this kind of spiritual practice with others. First, we all need each other's support, but especially during this kind of sacrifice. It's easy to abandon or quit, but it's very difficult when others' intentions are at stake. We can share and combine our fasting intentions for increased motivation. It works. In community, I like to read Scripture and discuss how we can influence or support the poor by our fasting.

When we fast, we are united with the hungry and now we can specifically unite ourselves with those less fortunate. One of my favorite charities to assist is Mary's Meals. Mary's Meals were named after the Mother of God. They provide over one million children in poverty-stricken countries with one meal per day as long as they spend time in the classroom being educated. To me, it makes perfect sense to fast for God's children.

Medical Benefits of Fasting

Here are a few medical benefits from an article from *John Hopkins Health Review Spring Summer 2016*. Mark Mattson is a professor of neuroscience at the Johns Hopkins School of Medicine and also serves as chief of the Laboratory of Neurosciences at the National Institute on Aging. According to the research conducted by him and others, cutting your energy intake by fasting several days a week might help your brain ward off neurodegenerative diseases like Alzheimer's and Parkinson's while at the same time improving memory and mood. Mattson explains that every time you eat, glucose is stored in your liver as glycogen, which takes about 10 to 12 hours to be depleted. After the glycogen is used up, your body starts burning fats, which are converted to ketone bodies, acidic chemicals used by neurons as energy. Ketones promote positive changes in the structure of synapses important for learning, memory, and overall brain health. But if you eat three meals a day with snacks between, your body doesn't have the chance to deplete the glycogen stores in your liver, and the ketones aren't produced.

The physical, medical and long-term effects of fasting have been and continue to be researched and studied by doctors and scientists throughout the world. "Scientists are only just beginning to discover and prove how powerful a tool it can be," says Dr. Michael Mosley who has written extensively on fasting, especially two days a week. The medical community says intermittent fasting has numerous health benefits, including weight loss, lower blood pressure, and reduced cholesterol.

Dr. Elaine Rancatore, DO, FACEP, IHC, one of the board members at Live the Fast, has been practicing emergency medicine for more than 18 years and works as an integrative health coach helping clients with behavior change to improve health. Dr. Rancatore is a strong proponent of fasting and has researched the medical benefits. They include: decreased cardiovascular risk factors, decreased blood pressure, decreased LDL cholesterol, decreased triglycerides, Increased HDL, Improved insulin sensitivity, decreased markers of inflammation, decreased markers of oxidative stress, and Increased longevity of life.

Dr. Elaine Rancatore has also found that fasting gives the digestive system a chance to rest and to do repairs. Specifically the liver has a chance to rest, because when one is fasting, the liver can focus on detoxification and breaking down toxins in the body. This is why it's important to stay hydrated when fasting. Dr. Rancatore encourages fasters to congratulate themselves on the commitment to fast and to begin slowly. You can watch her video on health benefits of fasting at livethefast.org.

One last point on the medical benefits: in 2011, Fox News featured a segment on fasting with Dr. Isadore Rosenfeld who said that, "cultures with fasting on a regular basis have fewer health risks than other people." Dr. Rosenfeld said that fasting may cut down the risk of heart disease and diabetes. He also said, "There is no question that regular fasting is good for you."

So what about medical issues? I can personally tell you that all fasting, whether a bread and water fast, fasting from TV or social media, fasting from your cell phone, these are pleasing to God.

During a talk in Chicago, I got this question: "What about my medical situation?" As I was waiting to answer this question, I felt in my heart Our Lady prompting me to tell them to fast from their schedule and spend time with my son in adoration and the benefit will be the same.

On the website CRU.org, founded by a great supporter of fasting, Bill Bright, it says all the experts agree that "breaking the fast" is the critical phase of fasting. While your body is in the resting mode, your stomach shrinks and your intestines become idle, so solid food must be re-introduced very slowly to avoid digestive distress. I usually break the fast with a very light meal, some soup or salad. Further, if you end your fast gradually, the beneficial physical and spiritual effects will last for days. You will start to look forward to the next fast day.

Throughout this book, we have described the spiritual reasons to fast, but these are only a few medical benefits.

It is important that one must consult their doctor and research this discipline themselves before taking this journey.

The best spiritual writing on fasting is the book, *Fast with the Heart,* by Father Slavko Barbaric. It is a wonderful fasting companion and outlines the basics and beginnings to a bread and water fast. We highly recommend reading it before or as you start fasting. Other fasting companions include: *The Spirituality of Fasting* by Monsignor Charles Murphy, *To Love Fasting* by Father Adalbert de Vogue, *Freed and Healed by Fasting,* by Sister Emmanuel Maillard, and the *2009 Lenten Message* by Pope Benedict XVI (PDF version available online).

These are drastic times that require drastic measures. So why not look to this discipline Jesus Himself used to prepare for significant events in His life and as a tool to cast out evil?

Questions
1. Because fasting provides both spiritual and physical benefits, do you understand now why Our Lady is asking us to pray and fast?

2. Can you understand why the consumption of certain foods we eat will prevent us from fasting and will create a desire for more?

3. Why do you think most people are hesitant to try fasting?

Chapter Eleven

Live the Fast Testimonials

*They appointed presbyters for them in each church and,
with prayer and fasting, commended them to the Lord
in whom they had put their faith. (Acts 14:23)*

Live the Fast is a Roman Catholic Apostolate founded in 2012 that is focused on bringing more awareness to the discipline of fasting by offering educational resources on prayer and fasting and a prayer community that will inspire one to "live the fast."

Over the past five years, *Live the Fast* has received numerous testimonials on the power of fasting in answering prayers and changing lives. Fasting *is* powerful! Here is a small sample of the many emails and letters we have received.

I have struggled with addictions my entire life. Over the years by the grace of God I have been able to beat all of my addictions with the exception of one: an addiction to lust and pornography. I had just about given up and then I heard your message on the radio. I have fasted now for about 30 days on Wednesdays and Fridays and have avoided all temptations. You are impacting souls. Thank you for listening to His call! (Keith)

When I started fasting, everything came alive to me. The colors were more vivid, the truths of the Catholic Church were so obvious that I wept that I did not see them previously. I wanted everyone to experience the joy and love I felt and to fall in love with Jesus in the Eucharist. Fasting has opened my spiritual eyes. (Marion)

I have prayed outside abortion centers infrequently for the last 5 years. Sometimes I fasted 24 hours before and during the shift. The days I fasted, I felt so much more peaceful and effective. The two "saves" were on my days of fasting. One of the women walked to my friend and me, crying and calling us angels, and fell into my arms. My other complete fast for 24 hours was for the stopping of a Black Mass. Many were fasting around the country. The Black Mass did not take place at Harvard area as was planned. (Anne)

I had a hard time forgiving a family member who has been verbally abusive to me for most of my life. It was only through fasting for this relative that I was finally able to forgive. It may not sound like a miracle, but in my eyes, it is most definitely a powerful testament to the power of fasting in my own life. Thanks so much!! (E.H.)

I just wanted to give my testimony of how fasting brought a miracle into my life. My father had Alzheimer's. I fasted for a week, just having bread and water for breakfast and lunch, but eating a regular modest dinner. The following week was Christmas and we would be all gathered together. At this point in his illness, my father could barely eat and drink, everything was making him choke. But a miracle happened, he was able to enjoy Christmas dinner. Not only that, but he recognized all of us, even the grandchildren. We really had our dad home with us for Christmas, and this was his last one with us. He died 8 months later. Prior to this miracle, I had fasted for him and his for 3 days. I didn't tell anyone about the fast. When I went to visit him, and we were alone in the room, he said to me, "I can't begin to thank you for what you did for me". He could never have known or understood what I did. It was a miracle. (Laura)

Live the Fast has had a huge and blessed impact on my life. Like any gift, sometimes we take it for granted. I still fall short, but when I pray about fasting and try to remember so many who have great trials and need my prayers, I start to see fasting as a gift and not a burden. It is a gift because it starts to make me more free and not a slave to my stomach. And then doors to graces start to swing wide open. Thank you for this gift! (Jim)

"I had a terrible relationship with a family member. She misinterpreted my love as being judgmental. I prayed, fasted and patiently waited. Our relationship is now 180 degrees different. I get to see my grandchildren and play with them. I'm told that I'm loved and appreciated. On fasting days I feel lighter and happier. My fast is not perfect. I try but since I work full time and have a somewhat physically demanding job I just fast until 4 pm." (J.M.)

"In all the years I have fasted never did I give up coffee. However this time was different. After a long dry spell from fasting, I decided to try again and asked for the grace to do so. I want to give all my fasts to our Blessed Mother for her intentions. She knows best what I recommend to her and she knows who is suffering the most in the world. The truth is, I was happy to find a bread that was not modified, healthy and natural. When I eat your bread, I think of the time when Jesus walked the earth with his apostles and when they were hungry, how happy they were to eat this bread. They are actually sharing their bread with me. Isn't that a joyful thought? You are so right that commercial bread makes you hungry. So this time for the first in all of my years of fasting, I made the decision for no coffee, only bread and water, just like Mary asks. I am so liberated now. I am a

big coffee drinker. I had so much energy and extra time. I took on little projects that have been on the back burner for a long time. Not only did I receive this blessing, but on my first Wednesday of fasting I wanted to wait until the mailman came with the fasting kit to eat the bread. Around 3:00 p.m. I was getting pretty hungry so I thought I will go into my bedroom first to pray the Chaplet of Divine Mercy, then have a piece of my store-bought bread to hold me over. On my way to my room I needed to do something outside so I opened the door and the mailman actually brought the fasting kit to my front door. Perfect timing!" (Linda)

Question

1. Pick one testimonial and contemplate/meditate and perhaps discuss with your friends and family the power and benefits of prayer and fasting.

Chapter Twelve

The Chaplet of the Holy Fast

*He (Jesus) said in reply, It is written: One does not live
by bread alone, but by every word that comes forth
from the mouth of God.* (Matt 4:2-4)

In June of 2014, my family moved to Framingham, Massachusetts to be in a one-floor ranch home and to be closer to our grandchildren. No one knew this, but my biggest concern was how I would attend Mass at Saint Clements in Boston 45 minutes away.

One morning in August of 2014, I attended the eight a.m. daily Mass at a parish in Framingham by the name of Saint Stephen's. I ran into my friend and adoration warrior, Elizabeth Mahoney, and she introduced me to a very holy priest, Father Francisco J. Anzoátegui, who was nicknamed Father Paco.

I had heard of Father Paco and his healing ministry and how Our Lord has given him special graces. I then realized he was the priest who had had a powerful role and intercession with the healing of one of our customers with a brain tumor. It just so happens that after we met, he gave me a blessing while on my way out of Mass. It became clear that this was not a normal blessing. I had been given hundreds of priestly blessings, particularly after founding the fasting ministry, but this one was different. The best way to describe it is that when his hands touched my head, the Holy Spirit penetrated my soul. As I walked out of church, I knew I needed to get to know this priest better.

Many months went by. I joined the Saint Stephen's Monday night prayer group and attended Father Paco's monthly healing masses. Saint Stephen's is a special bilingual parish with dedicated parishioners who love Jesus and each other. Father Paco is the pastor and spiritual leader to all who walk through the doors of this parish. He has a tremendous love for Our Lady, and he never says no to anyone. He is an exceptional priest and has become a close friend.

Monthly healing Mass starts on Monday night at seven p.m. and can last as late as eleven p.m. especially with hundreds of sick people being prayed over by Father Paco and his team. Many are slain in the spirit and left on the floor in front of the altar until they wake up. There are numerous people who are deathly sick, and I always feel like I ought to wait until the end for my blessing.

One night, after praying a few Rosaries for the sick, I approached the altar to be prayed over and receive a blessing. My friend Marge anointed my forehead with the holy oil as I found myself the last to be blessed. Father Paco embraced me with a big hug and then placed his hands on my head. During the blessing, he prayed faithfully to the Blessed Mother for her intercession in my life and my family. The blessing lasted about five to seven minutes. He then said, "I am going on pilgrimage to Fatima, Lourdes, and Garabandal in September and you need to come." It didn't sound like an invitation but a mandate. Father Paco was very firm and straightforward. I wasn't sure what it all meant.

In my life I had been to only one Marian site — Medjugorje — where I was able to receive my life confession. That led to an ongoing transforming conversion. (You can learn more about it in my first book, *From the Hub to the Heart*.)

I had read many books about these locations but really never thought about visiting them until Father Paco said that I must come. Having a devotion to the Blessed Mother and visiting these sites with Father Paco would make for a special trip. Besides, when I looked at the dates, I realized that we would be in Fatima exactly 100 years to the day from the time Saint Michael gave the visionaries the Holy Eucharist and prepared them for the coming of Our Lady. As I walked out of the healing Mass, Marge handed me a brochure for the trip. In a few days, I was booked and scheduled to visit Europe, to pray at three prominent apparition sites where the Mother of God had appeared.

Fatima in Portugal is one of the most celebrated apparition sites in the world. Our Lady appeared to three shepherd children: Lucia, Francisco, and Jacinta, between May and October of 1917. The last one, on October 13th, 1917 was witnessed by over 75,000 people, and it's the day when after a driving rainstorm soaked the ground and drenched the people, Our Lady and her Son performed the Miracle of the Sun. Each attendee — along with the ground — was bone dry within seconds of the Miracle of Sun. Several times in visits to Medjugorje, I have seen the spinning sun, but the rotating of the sun out of its access in the sky? To me, it was a clear indication that heaven was present.

We were in the process of boarding the bus from Fatima to get ready for a long ride to the next destination. Father Paco had informed me at some point after praying a Rosary that he would like me to come up to the front of the bus and give a teaching on Our Lady. I agreed and started my preparation on the talk. We were about two hours into the trip when we gathered for a rest stop and coffee.

The bus was very comfortable and filled with about 35 people from Massachusetts with a dedication to the Blessed Virgin Mary. We all boarded the bus and started praying the Rosary. At the conclusion, Father Paco signaled for me to come to the microphone at the front of the bus. My brothers and sisters on the bus seemed eager to hear another voice. I gave a teaching on the virtues of the Blessed Virgin Mary from a book on Saint Mother Teresa. At the conclusion, I was prompted by the Holy Spirit to give Father Paco a copy of an article I wrote on a different type of Rosary, one with fasting reflections. I felt very strongly that he had a direct line to heaven and Our Lady, so I wanted to get his feedback on this article and the idea for a fasting Rosary.

The next morning, I passed Father Paco at the breakfast buffet at the hotel. He told me that he studied and read my article during the night, and that he had some very important material from Our Lady on the holiness of the fast. He told me that once he prayed and reflected about it, he would share it with me.

The rest of the pilgrimage was one holy location after another, and it was really a reflection to me on how close heaven and all the angels and saints are to us here on earth. We arrived back in Boston during the last week in September of 2016, and I was eager to hear what Father Paco had to say about the fasting Rosary.

Autumn quickly transformed into the Thanksgiving holiday and the Holy Season of Christmas, and neither Father Paco nor I had the time to get together and talk.

What I didn't know was that Father Paco was carefully preparing a very holy writing and text that would influence the entire ministry of *Live the Fast*, and all those who were following Our Lady's call to fast for generations to come.

2017 is certainly a very significant year in the Church due to the 100-year anniversary of Fatima, but for me, it all changed with one communication from Father Paco that we should meet at the rectory on first Friday dedicated to Our Lady on January 6th, 2017. Father Paco would then reveal to me his reflections and thoughts on the fasting reflections.

I arrived at Saint Stephen rectory at seven p.m. for our appointment. Father Paco answered the door and, although he was walking gingerly from a bruised back, he escorted me to the parlor. He stated that he has injured his back, and I could see that he was not only sick with a cold but really in pain. He declared that his sickness, injury, or even evil temptations could not keep him from carrying out this message tonight. We started with a dedicated prayer from both of us to call upon the Holy Spirit and His most Sacred Spouse, Our Lady, for our time together, and to bless our family and friends. My heart was beating out of my chest in suspense for what he was about to say.

Father started by saying, "What I am going to give you is very sacred. Our Lady has chosen her day, the first Friday in the year of Fatima, to reveal all this to you. Remember we are both just a tool and this fasting project is hers." As Father Paco was speaking, I couldn't help but remember the similar words during my first-time conversation almost four years ago with Mother Olga when she said, "The Blessed Virgin Mary has been preparing me for this meeting with you. I want you to know that this is her plan, not yours; you're just the tool." These similarities of the setting and the conversation put me on notice to pay careful attention to all that was being shared and discussed.

Before handing me some paper, he shared his own feelings on what he was about to disclose. "Andy, when we talk about fasting today, you are Our Lady's apostle on fasting. I hear your passion and feel your knowledge on the topic, and it's inspiring what you have done over four years, especially for us priests. What I am about to give you is very scripturally-based and can be shared with all in the *Live the Fast* community. This chaplet is to be prayed on fast days to strengthen all those who fast. It was given to me in a dream from Our Lady, and that is why it took me so many months to get this to you. I wanted to pray and meditate on each word so I did not miss anything. No one — not even me — has prayed this prayer."

Father Paco smiled and handed me a paper entitled, "THE CHAPLET OF HOLY FAST." My mind was going a thousand miles per minute. Before we discussed the Chaplet prayer, I questioned him on the origin of the prayer and respectfully asked for clarification. He responded that while on pilgrimage to the Apparition sites after receiving my document on the Rosary and fasting, he had read it over. Then, Father Paco, after falling asleep, had a dream and the words along with the format of this prayer was the result. It is the property of the Blessed Virgin Mary. He confirmed to me that, yes, that is exactly what happened. "It's a special gift or grace to the world from Our Lady for you to market and get it out to the world. Andy, it's a pretty big task, but remember where it's coming from, and know that Our Mother will be with you each step of the way. I know you have been through this before and believe in your heart that she will direct you each step of the way."

After I heard this, my first thought was that this pilgrimage was filled with many graces, but that this was the reason I attended this trip.

Father Paco then handed me a copy of the prayer which he kept close to his heart for several months. "The Chaplet of the Holy Fast" is a prayer that while we are weak and try to fast, through prayer, Jesus will give us the strength to fast. It features Saint Michael and his prayer to cast out the evil spirits who destroy our lives. It also has a meditation on Saint John the Baptist fasting and praying for 40 days in the desert to prepare for the coming of Jesus. We are so busy in our own lives that we seldom prepare for anything, not even something as important as our encounter with Jesus.

After reviewing the prayers and discussing each meditation and word, Father Paco then tells me Our Lady's plan for this prayer. He states that in a few minutes tonight in his chapel at Saint Stephen in front of The Blessed Sacrament, "You should be the first to pray this prayer. After you pray it in the Chapel, I will then join you in prayer."

Second, he said that "Our Lady wants a bishop to give you an imprimatur for the chaplet."

Third, "You shall design a rosary specifically for the chaplet with purple beads for the Hail Mary beads and yellow or wheat for the Our Father beads. The crucifix is to be silver in color, and have a Saint Benedict Medal for protection. Then Our Lady would like you to bring it to the Holy Father."

When I think of the responsibility and the task ahead of us at *Live the Fast* ministry, I am grateful to know all things are possible with God.

As I was leaving Saint Stephen's rectory, I shared with Father Paco that this Chaplet of the Holy Fast will change lives and increase the pair of prayer and fasting. Fasting brings prayer to a whole different level of importance. By our fasting, we show God how serious our prayer really is.

I then mentioned to Father Paco that I need to send him a prayer that my spiritual director asked me to compose during retreat. When I got home, I emailed him the prayer, and then he added it to the end of the Chaplet. He said that "it shows the reader how dedicated your intentions are and how God is working in your life."

I have attached and copied the latest version of the chaplet for which Father Paco says each word has been reviewed and prayed fully discerned. Let each of us pray this chaplet especially on fasting days, share it with others, and retain in a journal or in your heart what it does for you spiritually each time you meditate on the mysteries. Thank You, Our Lady, for this gift and grace.

Start at the crucifix with the Sign of the Cross. (The power of the Cross enables us to unite our prayers to Jesus as He offers the ultimate sacrifice of love for humanity.)

First bead: The Apostles' Creed (We confess the faith in which we believe.)

Our Father....

Hail Mary....

Glory be....

Saint Michael the Archangel prayer. (Prayer to Saint Michael will enable us to fight all distractions as we try to pray, and all discouragement as we try to fast.)

First Mystery: Saint Joachim and Saint Anne fasted to conceive a child. (Briefly meditate on how the parents of our Blessed Mother fasted to be chosen for such a great privilege. Fasting is very pleasing in the eyes of God.)

Then, on each of the following ten beads repeat the phrase:
"Not by bread alone does man live, but by every word that comes from the mouth of God."

Second Mystery: Prophetess Anna fasted and prayed day and night in the temple. (Briefly meditate on the insights of prayer that we receive when we fast. We will grow in wisdom and knowledge.)

Ten times: **Not by bread alone....**

Third Mystery: John the Baptist fasted and prayed to prepare the way for the Messiah. (Briefly meditate how John the Baptist, the herald of our Savior, fasted and prayed in the desert and converted many souls to welcome our Savior. Even the hardest of hearts will convert through these two powerful means.)

Ten times: **Not by bread alone….**

Fourth Mystery: Jesus fasted for forty days and forty nights in the desert. (Briefly consider how our Lord and Savior fasted and prayed before He began his public ministry. He defeated temptation through fasting and began his ministry with great anointing.)
Ten times: **Not by bread alone….**

Fifth Mystery: Jesus teaches the value of fasting and prayer to his disciples. (Briefly meditate how Jesus teaches his disciples to pray and fast so that healings and miracles may happen through their intercession. Jesus continues to teach us today how to fast and pray.)
Ten times: **Not by bread alone….**

Returning to the last beads, say on the first bead:
Eternal Father, not my will, but yours be done!
I surrender to all that you want from me!
In the next three beads say:
I am the bread of life. He who eats my Body and drinks my Blood remains in me and I in him. (Three times)

On the last bead you say, **"Hail Holy Queen, Mother of Mercy….** To follow the advice that our Blessed Mother gave the first disciples at Cana in Galilee: *"Do whatever He tells you!"*
Make the Sign of the Cross again, and kiss the crucifix.

Purple beads: The color of penance….
Gold beads (or Yellow): The color of wheat and bread….
Silver Crucifix with the Saint Benedict medal: Penance is not a burden; it leads to a more joyful, fuller life in Christ.

A Prayer and Covenant Composed by Andy LaVallee
(while in front of Blessed Sacrament)

Lord and Creator, Guardian of my soul
and Father of all, please hear my prayer.
You have conquered sin and death.
The victory is yours and is already won.
May I be part of this victorious and heavenly celebration
to praise You for the graces and gifts that You have given to me.
I commit to You at this time, in the state of grace, after
receiving the Holy Eucharist and the Sacrament of Confession.
I give to You my entire life left for me to live on this earth.
To be the minister, the disciple, the apostle,
and the messenger of the truth of the Gospel
by taking the gift of time and focusing on the study,
the discipline, and the benefit of the team of prayer and fasting
that You have taught us.

To promote, encourage, and teach the discipline
to all those open to the words of Scripture
when you said, "When you fast...."
To encourage others, to commit resources,
to spread awareness of the discipline which you
yourself practiced, taught, and showed us all how to
cast out demons in our time today.

May the efforts of the *Live the Fast* ministry teach those who
fast the benefits of prayer and fasting as a team. Please bless all
those who fast, watch over and bless the staff and families who
honor you through "Live the Fast."

May the Blessed Virgin Mary stay close to all of us
as we follow her message to fast and pray.
May her Spouse, the Holy Spirit, guide the path of this ministry
so that we may honor and serve you.

Through the intercession of the Blessed Virgin Mary,
and all the Angels and Saints,
for the honor and glory of our Lord Jesus Christ. **Amen**

Acknowledgments

In dedicating this book to the healing of all families, I would like to acknowledge my own family. Giving thanks for: my wife of 42 years, Barbara, our son, Jeffrey, his wife Mian, and three children Sofia, Stella and Lucca; our daughter, Nicole, and her husband Joseph, along with their two children, Andrew and Lauren. We give Almighty God thanks for the gift of family and how they have all supported my activities.

I'd like to thank Darcie Nielsen for being our cofounder and partner as we grew the ministry of *Live the Fast*.

Father John Riccardo for his undivided commitment to fasting as a solution for our country.

Father Chad Ripperger for all the information he shared with us at the 2016 retreat at Our Sorrowful Mother's Ministry Retreat Center on the topic of fasting and why it is needed so much in this day and age.

Drew Mariani of Relevant Radio for his continued support and commitment to the discipline of fasting as a solution for all the challenges we face today within the world.

Ellen Gable Hrkach, *Live the Fast's* new Vice President, for all the work she puts into the Wednesday and Friday emails that help the entire *Live the Fast* community learn more about fasting every day. Also special thanks for editing and formatting this book.

To my friend, Father Paco, for agreeing to write the foreword for this book. His insight to the spirituality of fasting has been an inspiration to me.

Attorney Michael Gillis for his commitment to this ministry as the advisor and secretary to the executive board and, most of all, thank you for your friendship.

My friend Joe Falcao for his service to the executive board as *Live the Fast* treasurer.

Kathy Tierney for her flexibility and her commitment to make this ministry a success.

Iona Pasqual, who is the newest member of the *Live the Fast* team.

Tara Rohatgi, for always being there when we needed her to help, despite her responsibilities as a wife and mother.

Special thanks to an anonymous donor and his charitable foundation for the support they have regularly provided to keep *Live the Fast* an ongoing ministry.

My friend Scott Gieselman who has provided support and prayers to keep *Live the Fast* going. It's been a privilege to be the godfather of your son.

My life-long friend, Peter Belsanti, who shipped, packaged and served thousands of people through the ministry of *Live the Fast*. We wish him good health prior to his retirement years.

For the health and recovery of Father Michael Nolan, the spiritual director of *Live the Fast*, and we are grateful for his attitude and commitment to fasting and for agreeing to Wednesday adoration.

My friend Scot Landry who has reviewed every bit a piece of writing I have written over the years. Thanks so much for your feedback.

Dr. Elaine Racantore, who brings us the awareness of all the health benefits that go hand-in-hand with the spiritual benefits of fasting.

All of us at *Live the Fast* would like to thank the many priests, religious and deacons who promote prayer and fasting. We are especially thankful to our two priest board members, Fr. Tom Hart and Fr. Dermot Roache.

About the Author

Since 1969, Andy LaVallee, has been working in the bakery industry and in 1977, he started LaVallee's Bakery Distributors. LaVallee's is New England's premier provider of artisan breads and other bakery offerings to clients such as the InterContinental Boston, the Four Seasons, Boston College, and the Chateau Restaurants.

In recent years, during trips to Medjugorje, Andy grew to a deeper understanding of the practice of prayer and fasting, a practice that is common in this small village. He realized that he had a unique role, perhaps even a duty, to provide high quality breads to those in America who were interested in prayer and fasting. Andy has consulted with Sister Emannuel Maillard who wrote "Freed and Healed by Fasting," Fr. Charles Murphy author of "The Spirituality of Fasting" and others knowledgeable about the practices of a healthy fast and the ingredients of a fasting bread. He has also steeped himself in the teachings of the late Father Slavko Barbaric, who integrated into his many noble works, was his role as a humble practitioner and educator of prayer and fasting.

In Lent of 2012, we had a strong response to our initial LIVE THE FAST program. We gave out complimentary fasting breads and resources to many people who committed to stepping up their fasting during Lent. Our testimonials page features some of this feedback. Following this time, we decided to promote prayer and fasting throughout the year and launched our online service in November, in time for Advent.

Along with our educational resources, and opportunities to build community, we are excited to invite you to *Live the Fast*!

Andy's first book is *From the Hub to the Heart* and it tells his full conversion story.

References and Recommended Books

Barbaric, Fr. Slavko, *Fast With the Heart*, IC, Mir, Medugorje, 2000

Barbaric, Fr. Slavko, *Fasting, Live the Fast*, 2016

De Vogue Adalbert, *To Love Fasting: The Monastic Experience,* St. Bedes Pubns, 1994

LaVallee, Andrew, *From the Hub to the Heart*, *Live the Fast*, 2015

Murphy, Monsignor Charles, *The Spirituality of Fasting,* Ave Maria Press, 2010

Schmemann, Monsignor Alexander, *Great Lent*, *A Journey to Pasca,* St. Vladimir's Seminary Press; 2nd Revised edition

Thigpen, Paul, *A Year With the Saints,* St. Benedict Press, 2014

Endnotes

[1] Schmemann, Alexander, *Great Lent: Journey to Pascha,* St. Vladimir's Seminary Press; 2nd Revised edition

[2] Ibid

[3] Thigpen, Paul, *A Year With the Saints,* St. Benedict Press, 2014

[4] Miracles of the Saints website:
http://www.miraclesofthesaints.com/2010/10/miracle-of-eucharist-total-fast-from.html

[5] Mazza, Enrico and Lane, Ronald, *The Origins of Eucharistic Prayer,* Pueblo Books, 1995

[6] Milavec, Aaron, *The Didache: Text, Translation, Analysis, and Commentary,* Michael Glazer Publisher, 2003

[7] Aquilina, Mike, *The Time Capsule,*
https://fathersofthechurch.com/2006/05/23/the-time-capsule/ 2006

[8] O'Loughlin, Thomas, *The Didache: A Window on the Earliest Christians,* Baker Academic Publishers, 2010

[9] https://www.statista.com/topics/1141/health-and-fitness-clubs/

[10] Murphy, Monsignor Charles, *The Spirituality of Fasting: Rediscovering a Christian Practice,* Ave Maria Press *2010*

[11] De Sales, St. Francis, *Introduction to the Devout Life*, Image Classics, 1972

[12] De Vogue Adalbert, *To Love Fasting: The Monastic Experience,* St. Bedes Pubns, 1994

[13] Barbaric, Fr. Slavko, *Fast With the Heart,* First Edition, Medjugorje Web, 2012

[14] Ibid

Made in the USA
Monee, IL
02 March 2023

29014281R00070